Baby Let's Eat!

Baby Let's Eat!

by Rena Coyle

with Patricia Messing, Nutritionist

Foreword by Michael A. Levi, Pediatrician

Illustrations by Sandra Forrest

A Welcome Book

Workman Publishing, New York

For Catelyn

———

Library of Congress Cataloging-in-Publication Data
Coyle, Rena.   Baby, let's eat!
Includes index.   1. Children—Nutrition.   2. Cookery.
3. Menus   I. Messing, Patricia.   II. Title.
TZ361.C5C69   1987   641.5′622   86-40548   ISBN 0-89480-300-X (pbk.)

Cover and book design: Susan Aronson Stirling
Cover and book illustrations: Sandra Forrest

A Welcome Book

Workman books are available at special discounts when purchased in bulk for
premiums and sales promotions as well as for fund-raising or educational use.
Special editions or book excerpts can also be created to specification. For details,
contact the Special Sales Director at the address below.

Workman Publishing Company, Inc.
708 Broadway
New York, N.Y. 10003

Manufactured in the United States of America
First printing October 1987
10   9   8   7   6

———

Note: All children are unique and this book is not intended to substitute for the advice
of your pediatrician or other physician who should be consulted on dietary matters,
especially when your child is an infant or if there are any signs of illness.

Contents

Foreword

Parents in the 1980s are in the enviable position of being able to choose between breastfeeding and bottle feeding for their newborn babies. Whichever method is selected, infants grow and thrive, easily doubling their birth weight between four and six months. At around this age they also become developmentally ready to begin sampling solid foods—and decisions about nourishment will never again be as simple.

Most parents eagerly anticipate the time when they can start their children on "real food." But then, paradoxically, as soon as they get the okay, they are overwhelmed by anxiety and an unending number of questions: "What foods should I give Sarah?" "How much?" "When?"

As the baby grows and becomes exposed to a greater variety of foods, the concerns and questions also grow: "Nina never eats enough" and "Danny binge eats!" "How do I get Aaron to eat a balanced diet?" "Is he getting everything he needs?"

Baby Let's Eat! presents the answers to these and many other questions I hear almost every day in my practice of pediatrics. The authors begin with one important principle: It isn't necessary that your child eat totally balanced meals every day, three times a day . . . being flexible with your child's eating behavior can be difficult, but it is in the *best nutritional* interest of your child.

Solid scientific nutritional information is presented in a format directly related to each stage of development. The clearly written text is reinforced by imaginatively conceived drawings. And then the authors do something I have not been able to do for my patients: they translate good nutritional principles into pragmatic day-to-day menus. They have devised menus that are not faddish, but that use juice concentrates as natural sweeteners and discourage the use of salt and saturated fats—great-tasting, healthful, easy-to-prepare menus I have enjoyed preparing with my own children.

It is a pleasure to introduce you to this unique book, which will provide mothers and fathers with an invaluable reference source for nutritional information, and at the same time serve as a handy, indispensable, every day family cookbook.

Michael A. Levi, M.D., Ph.D.
Department of Pediatrics
New York University Hospital

A Word from the Authors

At no point in history have newborn babies been bigger or healthier than now. It's not just luck; it has to do with technological progress. Many factors are responsible: superior prenatal care for mothers, a fuller understanding of the developmental and birthing processes, and better nutritional practices among mothers-to-be who understand that "eating for two" is more than just eating twice as much. And so, for the better part of nine long months, mothers prepare for the arrival of their baby. A layette is assembled, parties are thrown, names are chosen and discarded, and plans for the future begin to take shape.

And then your baby is born. He or she is everything you wished and hoped for—happy, healthy, and *hungry*. Of course, in the beginning, feeding your child is relatively easy. Baby gets almost all of his or her nutrients from breast milk or formula. However, in a mere four to six months, baby is ready for more. But, how does one determine what and how much a new baby wants or needs to eat? Who knows? In desperation most parents reach for the familiar jars of prepared baby foods from the supermarket; others spend hours in the kitchen, slavishly trying to prepare perfectly balanced meals, made especially for baby. Relax. You really needn't go to such extremes.

This book will answer all the questions and waylay all the insecurities you'll ever have about the correct nutritional balance your baby needs. You'll be surprised at how easy it is to adapt the meals you make for the rest of the family to include its newest member.

THE GOAL OF THIS BOOK

Based on the most up-to-date nutritional information available, we have developed recipes that will give your baby the tastiest, most healthful foods and will also please your family and guests. From the first day your child begins to eat solid foods, his meals can be much the same as yours. If your own diet is not what it could or should be, this is the perfect time to lay down a new set of rules for everyone in the household. When you prepare vegetables for yourself, set aside a few spoonfuls to purée for baby. Save some leftover breakfast oatmeal to warm up for a snack later in the day. With almost no extra work from you, your child has the advantages gained from eating freshly prepared foods. Don't forget: A baby's sense of taste begins to develop with his first food experiences. So, when babies like flavor, they (like us) enjoy tasting it again and again. Isn't a passion for spinach, asparagus, or apples preferable to constant cravings for chocolate or ice cream or thick slabs of butter? Isn't spaghetti with a home-made tomato sauce more worthwhile than canned? Fresh foods do taste better than jarred,

canned, or dried. It's up to you—and completely within your ability—to "create" a child who prefers fresh foods to prepared foods; this is your chance to establish good lifelong nutritional habits. You'll know you have succeeded when you find your child enthusiastically reaching for the vegetables adults imagine kids hate!

Your child develops one step at a time, both inside and out. A baby smiles before he laughs; eating works very much the same way. First, a baby must drink formula or breast milk. As the throat muscles mature, the child can begin to swallow solid foods. At the same time, the digestive track becomes more and more capable of accommodating different kinds of foods. After formula or breast milk, babies can eat cereals, then vegetables and fruits.

Baby Let's Eat! will give you an overview of the nutritional needs of children under three. Handily, after the first six months, nutritional needs break down into four stages by age: six to 12 months, 12 to 18 months, 18 to 24 months, and 24 to 36 months. For every stage, we will provide a guide to the variety of foods your child will be able to eat and how to fit the preparation of these foods into the cooking you do daily for the rest of your family. We give you quick techniques for turning "table food" into baby's food.

(You'll learn too just how much nutrition your child gets from the foods you make.) And in following our suggested menus and recipes, you will develop a repertoire of dishes that both you and your baby will enjoy.

Undoubtedly the biggest challenge you will face here is omitting salt from your diet. The use of salt is an *acquired* habit, one that shouldn't be encouraged in developing children. In the recipes that follow we use the flavors of herbs, spices, and other seasonings to complement food, without adding any salt. In fact, salt and other forms of sodium are found in so many commercial foods that there is good reason not to add more to your lives and risk the long-term effects from overuse.

This book is directed to the nutritional needs and finicky tastes of children under three. Of course, it is not meant to substitute for advice from your pediatrician, who should be consulted on diet especially while your child is an infant. But it is filled with good recipes and sound information and we hope you'll keep using it long after your baby is out of diapers.

Rena Coyle and
Patricia Messing

CHAPTER ONE

Food and Your Baby

As children mature from infancy to toddlerhood and beyond, what they eat affects their growth, development, learning ability, and general behavior. Because of the rapid growth that takes place during these early years, infants and small children need ample supplies of nutrients. They need to be fed the correct variety of foods. It makes sense then, that the quality of the food given to your infant or toddler be of the highest nutritional value. Delivering the best requires attention to the Four Basic Food Groups: proteins, dairy products, fruits and vegetables, and cereals and grains.

Children pick up the eating habits of their parents. If parents don't favor lamb or asparagus, chances are children will not have the opportunity to find out if they do. If a mother or father has a sweet tooth, chances are the child could develop one due to the sweets that are kept as staples around the house. If your own diet needs an overhaul, the time is now. Make a few improvements for yourself while planning a healthy diet for your child. If adults are seen enjoying a variety of foods, children will learn to enjoy them. It's never too early to start your child on the road to good eating habits.

FROM THE START

All healthy infants require the same amounts of the same nutrients. Until the age of four to six months, your baby receives complete nutrition from breast milk or formula, or a combination of both. It is generally recognized that human milk best supports the growth of infants. Indeed, there are compelling arguments which favor the breastfeeding of infants, including the following:

- Human milk contains more easily digested proteins.

- There is less saturated fat in human milk.

- The antibodies in breast milk help the child fight disease.

- Breastfeeding promotes bonding between mother and child.

However, the breastfed baby may need daily supplements of vitamin D, iron, and fluoride (your pediatrician will prescribe whatever is appropriate). If your baby is formula-fed and the formula is adequately fortified, no supplementation may be necessary. Again, it's best to check with your pediatrician.

At six to twelve months, Baby is ready for more than just milk. Barley, oatmeal, and rice cereals, well cooked and very smooth, are first added to the baby's regimen. These then are supplemented with thin purées of mild vegetables, such as carrots, potatoes, green beans, and squash. Non-acid fruit juices and purées of apples, pears, or bananas can follow. Just remember that sharp citrus fruits are too strong for a child of this age.

By one year of age, your baby will be ready to eat real food—much like what the rest of the family eats. Interestingly, at this time the growth rate becomes slower, almost as though the baby is meant to grow experientially rather than physically. Now is a good time to widen the variety of foods you prepare for Baby. Don't expect miracles, though; tastes develop gradually. Appetites may appear to wane, but, in fact, few children actually need fewer calories. Meals may become erratic and your child may become a finicky eater. Don't panic! Just pay special attention to what your child *does* eat and be sure to keep healthful snacks on hand such as yogurt, fruit, crackers with peanut butter or cheese, soft-cooked vegetables with dip, muffins, or milk custards. This stage, too, shall pass.

THE BASICS

A few rules give you an idea of what good nutrition is all about—for your child, your family, and yourself. The Dietary Guidelines for Amer-

icans, published in 1980 by the United States Department of Agriculture, suggest that we:

- Eat a variety of foods.

- Maintain ideal weight.

- Avoid too much fat, saturated fat, and cholesterol.

- Eat foods with adequate starch and fiber.

- Avoid too much sugar.

- Avoid too much sodium.

All the nutrients your child needs are found in the foods we normally eat, but no single food provides all of those nutrients. Offer your child a variety of foods in small portions, introducing new ones at the same meal with a favorite food. Compliment your child for tasting a new food, but never reward or bribe a child with ice cream or cookies!

If your child eats a variety of foods, she will probably not have a deficiency or an excess of any nutrient. However, don't worry when your child refuses some foods. It isn't necessary that she eat totally balanced meals three times a day. Look at the balance of foods eaten over a week's time and determine whether or not the total intake is nutritionally well balanced. If your child refuses to eat chicken and carrots one night and wants only mashed bananas and milk, chances are good that sometime later in the week, she will eat proteins and vegetables. Young children need to experiment with food. Urging them to eat foods they do not like or forcing them to

eat when they are not hungry may set the stage for eating disorders or weight problems later in life. Being flexible with your child's eating behavior may be difficult for you (most of us were brought up having to clean our plates), but it is in the best nutritional interest of your child.

THE SPECIFICS

Nutrients are substances that promote growth and maintain health. The nutrient groups include: proteins, carbohydrates, fats, vitamins, minerals, and water.

Proteins: Proteins are made up of building blocks called *amino acids*. There are 22 amino acids that combine in different ways to make different proteins. Of the 22 amino acids, there are eight (or possibly nine) that our bodies cannot manufacture. These are called the *essential amino acids*. We must rely on foods to supply them to our bodies. Proteins from animal sources (meat, poultry, fish, dairy products, and eggs) supply all of these essential amino acids. For that reason they are called *complete proteins*. Vegetable sources of protein (grains, dried peas and beans, nuts and seeds) are *incomplete protein foods;* they contain only some of the essential amino acids. By combining vegetable proteins (rice and beans, for example) at the same meal, you can boost their nutritional value.

Our bodies need protein to build and repair tissue, to form antibodies to fight infection, and to give us energy. In young children, protein is vital for developing strong healthy bodies. If your child is eating some meat, eggs, peanut butter, or beans along with some dairy products, he is getting plenty of protein. A word of caution here: excessive intake of protein is not good. An overabundance of protein can include excessive fat—unhealthy at any age. Be reasonable about

the amount of protein your child eats. Give your child enough protein, but don't overdo it.

Carbohydrates: Carbohydrates as a group are subject to misconceptions. They are not fattening. Ounce for ounce, carbohydrates have fewer calories than high-fat protein foods such as beef or cheese. What matters about carbohydrates is the form they take. There are two types of carbohydrates: *simple* and *complex.* Simple carbohydrates are sugars, including table sugars, honey, molasses, corn syrup, and fruit sugars. Foods made with some of these sugars—candy, cake, pie, cookies, soft drinks, and many jams and jellies—contribute *empty calories* to a diet; they have calories but few—if any—nutrients. These simple carbohydrates are the ones that bear scrutiny in the everyday diet. (The sweets we suggest in this book use pure fruit juices as a sweetener, making them healthy alternatives to high-sugar snacks.)

Complex carbohydrates are found in starchy foods such as grains, dried peas and beans, pastas, and vegetables. These foods should make up a large part of your child's diet. Even though dried peas and beans are not necessarily favorites with small children, they are delicious—and popular—in dishes such as our Great White Bean and Red Bean Pie.

Carbohydrate foods are a good source of energy, some important vitamins and minerals (especially the B-complex vitamins), and often substantial amounts of fiber. Fiber is the indigestible part of plant foods, which provides bulk in the diet and works as a natural laxative. Everyone's diet should include generous amounts of fiber, and this is easily found in brown rice, oatmeal, whole-grain breads, pasta, fruits, and vegetables.

Fats: Some amount of fat is necessary in every diet, but most Americans, including children, eat far too many fatty foods. Young children need fat in their diets to develop the fatty insulation around nerve endings that promotes motor coordination. Therefore, use whole milk for weaning your child and continue with it until your baby is at least two years old. Use fats in moderate amounts in food preparation. Don't butter vegetables heavily, even though that's the way you love them. Promote moderation in your child's eating habits. The recipes in this book will help you.

Fats are either saturated or unsaturated. Saturated fats generally come from animal sources and are solid at room temperature. Butter, lard, and other meat and poultry fats are saturated fats. Coconut oil, palm kernal oil, and palm oil are saturated fats which come from plants. Saturated fats tend to raise blood cholesterol levels and increase the risk of heart disease. Check packaged foods to see what kind of fats are used in their preparation. As a rule, it is best to limit the amount of saturated fats in the diet.

Unsaturated fats—monounsaturated or polyunsaturated—come primarily from plants. Polyunsaturated fats have been shown to reduce cholesterol levels in the blood. Good sources of polyunsaturated fats are safflower, sunflower, corn, cottonseed, and soybean oils and margarine, which has oil as a primary ingredient.

Monounsaturated fats are found in olives, olive oil, peanut oil, and peanut butter.

To minimize fat in your child's diet, buy extra lean meats and trim away the fat. Broil, bake, braise, or sauté meat, poultry, and fish; frying adds too much fat. A few drops of good olive oil sprinkled on vegetables or fish can bring an unexpected, more healthful, taste payoff.

Vitamins: Vitamin deficiencies are rare in American children. If your child regularly eats food from the Four Basic Food Groups (see chart, page 18), he probably gets enough vitamins. Vitamins often don't survive in overcooked foods, especially in vegetables. So, if you are at the thin purée stage with your eight-month-old, don't cook vegetables until they are mushy. Cook them until crisp-tender and let your blender or food processor turn them into mush. By one year or so, you'll be able to mash the vegetables sufficiently with the back of a fork.

Vitamins A and D are particularly important to growing children. Yogurt, cottage cheese, and other dairy products may not be fortified with vitamins A and D; check the package labels. Be sure that your child drinks fortified milk, or that he gets vitamins from other sources.

Minerals: Two minerals especially important to a growing child's diet are calcium and iron. Calcium is needed for bone formation and growth. Requirements vary from 360 milligrams a day for infants to 800 milligrams a day for toddlers. Dairy foods are the best sources of calcium. Two cups of milk plus the calcium found in in other foods eaten over the course of the day easily provide the 800 milligrams. (If your child cannot tolerate milk, see Milk Sensitivity and Lactose Intolerance, page 22.)

Iron, essential for healthy blood and muscles, is found in liver, red meat, fish, egg yolks, green leafy vegetables, dried fruit, whole-grain or enriched breads, cereals, and cooked dried beans. Without enough iron, your child may develop iron-deficiency anemia. This can occur at approximately six to nine months, and again at 18 months if a child's diet is composed largely of milk and other foods with a low-iron content.

Vitamin and Mineral Supplements: Vitamin and mineral tablets are *not* a substitute for a good diet. Megadoses of certain nutrients—especially fat-soluble vitamins such as vitamin A—may even be hazardous to your child. They are stored in the body and can build up to toxic levels. There is no evidence that healthy children eating normal diets need vitamin and mineral supplements. Never give your young children supplements except under your doctor's direction—no matter what vitamin commercials on television report.

Water: Water is a critical nutrient often overlooked in infant and child nutrition. Humans can survive only a few days without water. Babies need *lots* of water, so be sure to offer it periodically between feedings instead of milk. On hot days, keep your children well hydrated with water rather than with sugared drinks that don't hydrate or cool the body as quickly. If your child suffers from diarrhea, which can contrib-

ute to dehydration, urge him to drink plenty of fluids such as club soda or "pedialyte" (a commercial preparation) to replenish water as well as sodium.

THE BIG PICTURE:

All right, now you know everything you need to know about nutrients. But kids don't eat nutrients—they eat food: milk and milk products, meat and meat alternatives, fruits and vegetables, breads and cereals. Use this book to get an idea of the variety you can offer your child, but don't panic if your child refuses some of your offerings. It isn't necessary to meticulously balance each of your child's meals.

Our menus are based on the Four Basic Food Groups, and many of the recipes include

FOUR BASIC FOOD GROUPS: CHILDREN AGES 1 TO 3 YEARS OLD

Food	Suggested Serving Size	Recommended Daily Serving
Milk and Milk Products		2 to 3 servings
Milk	1 cup	
Yogurt	1 cup	
Cheese	1 ounce	
Cottage cheese	½ cup	
Meat and Meat Alternatives		2 or more servings
Lean meat, fish, poultry	2 to 3 tablespoons	
Eggs	1 whole	
Cooked dried peas or beans	1 to 3 tablespoons	
Peanut butter	1 to 2 tablespoons	
Fruits and Vegetables		4 or more servings total
Vitamin C: citrus fruit or juice, tomatoes, broccoli, bell peppers, berries	1 to 3 ounces juice 2 to 6 tablespoons solids	1 or more servings

Note: Fats such as oils, margarine, butter, and mayonnaise may be used in small amounts, totaling 1 to 2 teaspoons, daily.

foods from three or four of these groups. Each group doesn't need to be represented individually in the diet. Think about it. Every time you have a bowl of cereal with milk and sliced bananas, you are eating from three groups at once.

Confusion can set in when a new mother or father is faced with how much to feed his or her child. Some servings look so minuscule, you think the baby could never survive on such a tiny amount of food. A good rule of thumb for serving sizes of meats, fruits, vegetables, and grains is to offer your child one tablespoon of each food for each year of life. It is better to give small portions and let your child ask for more. Don't heap your child's plate and expect her to finish everything. The "Clean Plate Club" is not the goal; a well-fed, healthy baby is.

Recommendations for serving sizes from the Four Basic Food Groups for children one to three years appear above.

CREATIVE NUTRITION

We once knew a family that ate the same dish on the same day of the week, every week of the year. It was a case of, "If it's Tuesday, it's Meat

Food	Suggested Serving Size	Recommended Daily Serving
Fruits and Vegetables, con't.		**4 or more servings total**
Vitamin A: dark green and deep yellow fruits and vegetables including broccoli, carrots, pumpkin, sweet potato, apricot, cantaloupe, spinach	1 to 3 ounces juice 2 to 6 tablespoons solids	1 or more every other day
Other fruits and vegetables		As desired to meet daily needs
Breads and Cereal		**4 or more servings**
Whole-grain or enriched bread	½ to 1 slice	
Cooked cereal, rice, pasta	2 to 6 tablespoons	
Dry cereal	½ to ¾ cup	

Loaf Day." The children in the family would do anything to be invited for dinner at a friend's house. They just couldn't bear the regularity and the boredom of the meals they were served at home. Creativity is important in feeding your child, so arrange the food attractively on the plate and make sure there is variety from day to day. Take advantage of what fruits and vegetables are in season; Mother Nature is an expert when it comes to variety.

Plan meals to include foods from each of the food groups. In each chapter for children over one, we include weekly menu selections to help

you. Breakfast might be an egg, milk, toast with a little margarine or butter, and fruit or juice. This would start your child off with a selection from each of the Four Basic Food Groups. Or serve our Oatmeal Pancakes with Chunky Pear and Apple Sauce and a glass of milk. You'll have wonderful breakfasts of almost infinite variety if you can use the food groups for inspiration. If your child would rather have pancakes for dinner and spaghetti for breakfast, it won't make any difference to her nutrition. In fact, it might be easier for you to reheat leftovers from last night's dinner than to start cooking first thing in the morning. Your child's refusal of breakfast food at breakfast time may temporarily jangle *your* nerves but remember that flexibility is important. If you are seriously concerned about your child's eating habits, keep a daily record of when and what your child eats over the course of a few days, then check this against the Four Basic Food Groups. You may be surprised. Your finicky eater can be getting her protein from cheese or peanut butter at snack time, even while refusing meat at meals. If so, prepare meals that concentrate on the remaining food groups.

A FEW REMINDERS

A baby's body is not developed enough to digest the protein from cow's milk before one year of age. After one, you may add cow's milk, but be sure it is whole milk only. The fat in whole milk is important in the development of necessary cushions around the body's nerve endings. Once

a child is two, it is all right to add low-fat and skim milk. When using yogurt or cottage cheese as a milk substitute, remember that these products are not fortified with vitamins A and D.

GOOD EATING HABITS: BORN OR MADE?

Little is known about why children eat what they do. We don't know why most children go through periods of favoring certain foods and refusing others. We do know a few things about some very specific tastes. All babies are born with a sweet tooth, an indifference to the taste of salt, and an aversion to bitterness. Individual food preferences and dislikes begin developing almost from day one. Many factors contribute to forming children's tastes in food: their parents' and siblings' examples, their own food experiences, and television are just a few. Many children consider cooked vegetables "yucky" because they like food that is chunkier and crisp-

er. Children will often eat raw those same vegetables that are a turn-off when cooked. Almost any vegetable may be served raw or lightly steamed to preserve crunchiness and nutrients. Try our Steamed Carrots, celery sticks, or cucumber spears with Sticky Dip.

Pressuring children about what they eat can lead them to devalue certain foods (like spinach) and place unfortunate emphasis on others (like sweets). Once children view green vegetables as the things they eat to get ice cream, it is difficult to change their minds. If you have this problem with your child, start offering the vegetables without pressure and without bribery. Compliment the child when he tastes a new food. De-emphasize sweets and begin incorporating naturally sweet fruits and moderately sweet baked goods into your child's diet. The Peanut 'n' Jam Squares, Sesame Crunch Cookies, or Orange Muffins easily can satisfy a sweet tooth. Older children and adults will love them too, and you can feel assured that these snacks are nutritious as well as mouthwateringly good. Remember too that tastes can change. The foods your baby hated at one year old might taste pretty good after a year of further tasting experiences.

WHAT ABOUT SALT?

You'll be happy to know that none of the recipes in this book contains added salt. The food is seasoned with herbs and spices, such as rosemary, dill, basil, mustard, and sesame seeds. There is no need to add salt to your child's food. The amount of sodium considered safe and adequate for a one- to three-year-old is what is found in approximately ¼ teaspoon salt. It's easy to get that amount naturally in foods without adding salt. Although salt has been omitted from commercially prepared puréed baby and junior foods, the amounts in toddler food are still generally high. Remember, too, that canned broth, canned vegetables, and canned vegetable juices are usually high in salt. If your child somehow has already learned to love salt, gradually decrease her intake, and use herbs and spices, lemon juice, and sesame seeds to add more zip.

SNACKS OR MEALS?

Do you remember being forced as a child to eat dinner at 6 PM just because that was mealtime? You were supposed to be hungry at that hour. What do you ask of your own children? Are they expected to be hungry at 8 AM, noon, and 6 PM, or do you let them eat when they are hungry? Children will usually listen to their bodies and request food when they are truly hungry. They have not yet learned to eat in response to anger, frustration, stress, boredom, and the host of other emotions that may trigger eating in adults. Let your child follow his internal hunger cues; it needn't create havoc in your home. If your child seems hungriest at 4 PM, give him his dinner at that time. He can have a healthy snack later, or when the rest of the family eats. By having extra meals in the freezer, you will always be prepared. Don't rearrange your whole family's schedule around a child's erratic eating behavior, but do listen for and respond to true hunger signals.

THE OVERWEIGHT CHILD

Overfeeding can be as serious a problem with children, as it is with many adults. However, it is also dangerous to make your baby or young child lose weight by underfeeding. The best way to deal with an overweight child is to slow the rate of weight gain so the child will grow into a normal weight as his length and overall body size increases. Review your child's eating habits and cut down on empty calories such as highly sugared foods; watch portion sizes and don't insist your infant finish his bottle.

If your child is overweight, pay careful attention to his activity level and see how you might incorporate lots of active play into the daily routine. Even babies can exercise by waving their arms and legs, crawling, and turning over. Sedentary children may become obese even when their food intake is not excessive, so get your kids moving and have fun with exercise! You may find yourself feeling better and more energetic in the process!

MILK SENSITIVITY AND LACTOSE INTOLERANCE

Milk sensitivity (or allergy) is sensitivity to the proteins in cow's milk, most often to whey or casein (although there are others). The condition ranges in severity from very mild to occasionally fatal. Symptoms may include skin rash, vomiting, diarrhea, or asthma. It tends to be milder in infants who have been breastfed. In cases of extreme sensitivity, the child must have a totally milk-free diet. In many cases, it is not a permanent condition. For infants, milk replacements include predigested or synthetic protein solutions on the market. Toddlers who need completely milk-free diets will get calcium supplements prescribed by the pediatrician.

Lactose intolerance (often referred to as "acquired lactose intolerance") is a fairly common condition in one- to two-year-old children. They cannot digest milk because of a deficiency in an enzyme which breaks down milk sugar. Lactose intolerance is often a temporary condition lasting two to three months. Symptoms include gas, bloating, cramps, and diarrhea. If your child has this condition, she may be able to tolerate small amounts of milk taken slowly with other food, though, in some cases, a child must avoid *all* milk products.

In some dairy foods, the milk sugar is already partly broken down and may be better tolerated. You can test your child with small amounts of yogurt with live cultures (check the label), buttermilk, sour cream, acidophilus milk, and aged cheese, like Cheddar, Swiss, and colby.

Fortified soy milk can also replace milk. You can purchase a brand of milk called Lact-Aid, which contains the enzyme "lactase," needed to break down milk sugar. The enzyme is also available in packets, ready to be added to regular milk.

Should you find that your child cannot tolerate any dairy products, you *must* carefully read all labels. Check the ingredients for milk solids, casein, whey, curds, or cheese solids. It may help to know that any food product marked "parve" contains no milk products.

Children may experience other food sensitivities: eggs, wheat, citrus fruit, and other foods or food additives. See your pediatrician if you notice unusual symptoms.

BROWN FOOD/WHITE FOOD

Research has shown us that whole-grain products are more nutritious than those that are processed in some way. But, for some unknown reason, many children object to the brown color of foods such as whole-wheat bread, brown rice, and bran muffins or cereals. It's best to introduce whole grains gradually, mixing brown rice with white, for example, and gradually increasing the amount of whole-wheat flour used in baking. Some children will enjoy a brown and white sandwich: one slice of white bread and one slice of whole wheat. Another good trick is to cook brown rice in chicken stock. When cooked, the rice turns yellow from the stock and virtually no one—even adults—will know that you started out with brown rice. Use whatever works for your child.

IS CAFFEINE OKAY?

Keep children away from caffeine. It is an addictive, stimulant drug found in coffee, tea, brown-colored colas, and sometimes in other soft drinks. Check labels. Your kids don't need it, and you could be setting up bad habits.

SUGAR EXCHANGES

When you're making desserts, remember that sweet does not always mean sugar! Other foods

Pass the Marjoram, Please

This guide will help you make the best flavoring choices when preparing your recipes, salt free!

Chicken: Rosemary, caraway seeds, coriander, curry powder, dill, marjoram, oregano, thyme, sage

Beef: Bay leaf, cinnamon, cumin, dill, fennel, marjoram, tarragon

Lamb: Rosemary, caraway seeds, coriander, curry powder, dill, marjoram, oregano, mint, fennel

Pork: Caraway seeds, cloves, sage, cumin, coriander, oregano

Fish: Clove, coriander, dill, fennel, rosemary, sage, tarragon

Vegetables: Basil, bay leaf, cumin, curry power, dill, marjoram, rosemary

Grains: Bay leaf, cloves, rosemary, basil, oregano, thyme

Baking: Cardomom, cinnamon, nutmeg, allspice, ginger, mace, clove, mint

can give a sweet taste and are not as nutritionally empty as sugar is. Use frozen fruit juice concentrates (apple, orange, and pineapple are the easiest to find), or stir in minced dried fruits such as raisins, figs, pears, apples, apricots, and pineapples.

CAUTION FOODS

Certain foods, when not mashed, chopped, or finely ground, may present danger of choking to infants or young children. These include:

    Nuts
    Olives
    Popcorn
    Sunflower seeds
    Uncooked peas
    Corn kernels
    Hot dog slices
    Chips (banana, corn, potato)
    Pieces of raw carrot or other hard
      vegetable
    Grapes
    Cherries
    Raisins

    As a special precaution, do not give honey to children under one year of age. It may contain botulism bacteria. For reasons that are unclear, these bacteria do not affect adults but can cause severe food poisoning in children under one.

COOKING FOR YOUR CHILD

Cooking Vegetables and Fruits: Vegetables and fruits are the first solid foods children eat. Here are some basic hints that you may want to keep in mind.

- Use fresh vegetables and fruits for the best flavor and to maximize vitamins and nutrients.

- Fresh-frozen, vegetables can be held for about two months before losing too many vitamins and too much flavor.

- Always wash your fruits and vegetables just before cooking. Do not assume that they have been cleaned by anyone else.

- Unpeeled fruits and vegetables retain more vitamins than peeled, so try to scrub skins well and avoid peeling when possible. Vitamins are found close to the skin.

- Cut fruits and vegetables into uniform sizes to ensure even cooking.

- To keep the vivid color of fresh fruits and vegetables, add a little acid—lemon juice or vinegar—to the cooking water. Don't forget that color counts to a baby; the food should look appetizing.

Steaming is the best method for cooking most vegetables because it ensures nutrient retention. The exceptions are parsnips and other fibrous root vegetables. Rinse your vegetables and peel them if necessary. Cut them into uniform pieces (about ½-inch thick), and place them in a bowl (if using a microwave oven) or in a steaming basket (for stovetop cooking). Place the steamer in a saucepan and add only enough water to create steam when brought to a simmer. The water should not touch the bottom of the steamer basket. Cover the saucepan and cook until just fork tender. The steaming time will depend on which vegetables you are cooking. Do not overcook; even crisp vegetables can be puréed or mashed fairly easily.

Braising is a method often used to cook vegetables such as cabbage, lettuce, endive, or thinly sliced root vegetables. It means long, slow cooking in liquid. You may use any liquid, from chicken or vegetable stock to water; the more flavorful the braising broth, the more flavorful the cooked vegetables will be. Wash and trim the vegetables. Partially fill a saucepan with the braising liquid and bring it to a simmer. Add the vegetables and check that they are about half-covered with liquid. If not, add more liquid. Cover the pan and let simmer until the vegetables are tender.

Panning or wilting is a wonderful way to cook spinach and other tender leaf greens. Wash and trim the greens thoroughly and shake them, leaving water droplets on the leaves. Place the leaves in a non-aluminum saucepan, cover it, and set over medium-high heat. As the pan heats, the water on the leaves will cook the vegetables. If you wish, add a little vinegar—try balsamic or tarragon-flavored—to the steaming liquid. It will perk up the flavor of the greens.

COOKING MEATS, POULTRY, AND FISH

The best cooking method depends on the cut you

are preparing. As a rule, the less expensive the cut, the longer it takes to cook.

Dry Cooking: Roasting and broiling are both methods of "dry" cooking. No additional fat or other liquid is added to the pan. When roasting meat, keep in mind:

- Meat should be at room temperature before cooking.

- Quickly searing-smaller pieces of meat or chicken in a skillet over high heat seals in its juices before roasting.

- Placing meat on a rack prevents it from poaching or frying in its own melted fats and juices.

- A lower roasting temperature (325°F is ideal), insures better flavor and texture of a dish.

- A meat thermometer most accurately reads internal temperatures of meat.

- The larger the cut, the longer it takes to cook.

- Meat continues to cook for 10 to 15 minutes after you remove it from the oven.

For larger cuts of meat or chicken, preheat the oven to 450°F. Cook the meat for 15 minutes. The outside of the meat will be seared, creating a surface that will keep the juices and flavor trapped inside. To make roasted meats even more flavorful, cut carrots, celery, and onions into ½ inch pieces. Make a layer of the vegetables in the bottom of a roasting pan. Place the seared meat on the vegetables. During the roasting, the vegetables will caramelize, adding a wonderful sweet flavor to your roast. (These vegetables are added to flavor the meat. Because they absorb so much of the fat, they should not be eaten.)

If you are baking fish, add a small amount of liquid to the pan to help keep the fish from drying out. Place the fish on a bed of cut vegetables such as carrots and fennel to add a little extra flavor.

Broiling cooks meat, poultry, and fish very quickly. The high heat sears the flesh and keeps the juices inside.

- Meat should be at room temperature.

- Trim off all fat.

- Broil the meat on a rack or broiler pan, so the melted fats drain away from the meat.

- Broil 3 to 5 inches from the heating coil.

- If your broiler is in the oven, keep the oven door open to let the steam escape, and prevent it from toughening the meat.

Cooking with Fat or Liquid: *Sautéing or stir-frying* are other popular and quick methods of cooking. They are nutritious if only a small amount of fat is used. All you need is a hot skillet, a small amount of butter or oil, and some thin slices of meat or fish. Cook until just translucent; overcooking will toughen meats unnecessarily, as will the addition of liquids.

Poaching is a favorite method for cooking chicken and fish as well as fruits and some vegetables. It keeps the finished dish moist. The key to delicious poached foods is in the poaching liquid. Bring a flavorful broth to a boil and add the chicken or fish. The liquid should cover the food completely; if it floats in the broth, invert a dish over the food to keep it submerged. Return the broth to a gently rolling boil and then reduce the heat to a simmer. Cook the fillets for the length of time given in each recipe. If you are poaching a whole fish or large fish fillet, wrap it in plastic wrap or cheesecloth to keep it from flaking apart while it cooks.

Poaching is a great method of cooking for

whole fruits such as pears or peaches. Again, if you use a flavorful liquid—apple or grape juice—you will end up with better tasting results.

Stewing means to cook slowly in a flavorful broth. Cut the ingredients into 1-inch cubes. Brown meat or chicken first in a little vegetable oil in a skillet or large kettle to caramelize the surface and give extra flavor and color to the stew. Next add the broth and any vegetables that need a long time to cook. Bring the liquid to a boil on top of the stove, then reduce the heat so that the liquid only simmers. Cover the pot and allow the stew to cook over low heat or in a preheated 325° to 350°F oven. Cook slowly until the meat becomes fork tender. Add the quicker cooking vegetables in the last 30 minutes of cooking time.

The Cool Down: There are two ways to cool cooked meats for storing in the refrigerator or freezer. The idea is to cool the meat fast so that bacteria do not have a chance to develop in the food. One way is to place the hot meat uncovered in the refrigerator to let much of the steam escape. Once it is cooled, cover it and freeze, if desired. The second method is to cover the meat and leave it on the counter for 1 to 1½ hours, then refrigerate or freeze. If your kitchen is warm, I recommend the first method.

PUREEING, MASHING, AND CHOPPING

Choose the cooking method that is right for the food you are preparing, then make it kid-ready.

For the brand-new eater the foods should be

cooked until soft, then purée until completely smooth. If any lumps remain, strain the purée. Most fruits and vegetables have enough natural moisture to make a smooth purée, so adding additional liquid is not necessary. The young eater will want to try one new taste at a time from a range of puréed vegetables or fruits. Remember, purées can be easily prepared from the main family meal.

Feed your child the same new food, without adding any others, for a few meals in a row and check for any reactions. Once he has eaten and enjoyed a few different fruits and vegetables, you can make them into all kinds of interesting combinations.

When your child graduates to meat and other protein foods, you may find it necessary to add a bit of formula, milk, or water to the purée to make it smooth. More advanced eaters won't need the extra step of straining; blending or processing will be enough. Now you can really enjoy the art of creative combinations! Perhaps liver by itself is not so popular with your child, but add a few spoonfuls of puréed pears, then stand back and watch. By mixing one of your child's favorite foods with another not as high on the list, you may get him to enjoy both.

Once a child is about nine to ten months old, foods will no longer need to be quite so smooth. A few small lumps will now be manageable by your small child. Any food that is naturally soft or has been cooked soft can be easily mashed with the back of a fork or spoon. Before your child reaches his first birthday, he will be able to manage food that has been cut into tiny pieces. Use food from the family dinner

and cut it into ¼-inch pieces. As your child grows, the size of the pieces can gradually get larger.

THE MACHINES

In the past, puréeing foods was time-intensive and tedious, with the hand-cranked food mill just about the only utensil available. Our choices today seem endless. Full-size and mini food processors are made in a wide variety of sizes. The standard size may be too big for every kitchen counter to sport comfortably, but the mini models take up less counter space than a toaster. When you need a quick purée, they can't be beat. Prices for large and small food processors are highly competitive; many minis are available for around $30 and are among the best investments you can make for your child.

Blenders may not be as popular now as they once were, but they do a fine job of puréeing foods. Remember, though, work in small batches; many blenders purée only the food around the blades, so you must stop and stir the food to ensure an even purée.

THINKING AHEAD

True convenience is always having a meal handy. When dinner is over, purée any of the leftovers that your child enjoys. If she is only

---

WHAT'S AVAILABLE WHEN

Many of these foods are available year round. Here is a chart of the peak seasons for the majority of fruits and vegetables grown and shipped in the United States.

Fall	Winter	Spring	Summer
Apples	Broccoli	Artichokes	Apricots
Avocados	Cabbage	Asparagus	Beets
Brussels Sprouts	Celery	Bananas	Berries
Cauliflower	Chinese Cabbage	Cabbage	Cherries
Celery	Eggplants	Carrots	Corn
Cranberries	Grapefruit	Greens	Cucumbers
Eggplants	Greens	Peas (early and	Grapes
Papayas	Oranges	snap)	Mangoes
Pears	Parsnips	Peppers	Melons
Potatoes	Peas (late winter)	Pineapples	Nectarines
Pumpkins		Rhubarb	Okra
Sweet Potatoes		Strawberries	Peaches
Turnips			Pears
Winter Squash			Peas (snap)
			Peppers
			Plums
			Summer Squash
			Tomatoes

tight bags or heavy-duty aluminum foil. They will be fine for up to two months.

Another good freezing method is to transfer cubes to special bags that are sealed closed with a heating device. When you are ready to reheat a meal frozen in one of these bags, simply drop it, unopened, into boiling water for about 15 minutes.

Still another way to freeze is to pour puréed foods into clean wide-mouthed jars and close tightly. If you seal foods well, you can keep water vapors from collecting around the food. Label the packages with the name of the food and the date on which it was frozen.

THAWING AND REHEATING

Frozen foods lose nutrients as they thaw. Therefore, the best thawing method is the fastest one, the one that will preserve the most food values. The best way to thaw any frozen food is in a microwave oven. If you own one, keep the food frozen solid until you want to cook it. Then, take it from the freezer, place in the oven and defrost according to the directions that came with your oven.

If you don't own a microwave, place the frozen food in the top of a double boiler and heat slowly over simmering water. Or place frozen food in a small heat-proof bowl and set it into a shallow pan of boiling water. It is always best to let food thaw over indirect heat, so that it will not scorch or burn in the pan.

starting on solids, keep the purées simple, but if she's already familiar with a variety of tastes, mix together any combination that sounds good. Broccoli and cauliflower, for example, or carrots and peas, potatoes and gravy. Then freeze the purées in individual serving containers. You can spoon puréed food into ice cube trays, cover, and freeze. Once frozen, transfer the cubes to air-

CHAPTER TWO

Your Child from 6 to 12 Months

As your child reaches four to six months, his throat muscles will be developed enough to begin swallowing solid food. Your pediatrician will let you know when to begin giving your child his first tastes. It's best to start with iron-fortified infant cereals made from rice, oats, or barley mixed with enough breast milk or formula to make the cereal almost liquid. (It may be tempting to offer something tastier, such as strained fruit, but fruit has no protein and may encourage a sweet tooth if given too early.)

Rice is least-often allergenic and a good beginning. Spoon some cereal into your baby's mouth and watch; babies' reactions vary. Yours may refuse the cereal entirely or leave it sitting in his mouth, not knowing what to do with it. Never fear, sooner or later, your baby will swallow. Once the food goes down, try another spoonful. Eventually, although not necessarily during your first attempt, the baby will open his mouth when he sees the cereal approach! When your child is comfortable with the spoon and cereal, begin making it slightly thicker.

Let your baby's appetite determine how much he eats, but don't force big quantities. Start with 1 to 2 teaspoons of cereal each meal and gradually increase the amount to 1 to 1½ tablespoons.

Even as you feed your child cereal in these early days, most of his nutrition still comes from breast milk or formula. The baby will gather nutritional benefit from solid

POINTS TO REMEMBER

Cooking for your six-month-old is different than cooking for adults. Keep in mind the following points:

- Until your baby is accustomed to eating, his food must be strained and almost liquid.

- Begin introducing new foods mixed with the familiar taste of formula or breast milk.

- When preparing a dish for the entire family, put aside the baby's portion before you add any strong spices.

- Introduce one new food at a time and check for any allergic reactions.

- Freeze any just-cooked-and-puréed foods as soon as possible. Whether you freeze in cubes or sealed jars, mark the packages clearly with dates and contents.

- You can adapt many of your own favorite recipes for baby by exchanging sugar with fruit juice concentrate or natural sweeteners. Hold off on the salt.

Your baby's first foods must be softened by cooking. Later, soft fruits and vegetables, such as pears, peaches, and cucumbers, can be puréed raw. A child of eight or nine months can eat many foods uncooked and with minimal puréeing.

foods here and there, but solid foods are not yet a staple. As your child grows and a variety of solid foods becomes a regular part of his diet, he will drink less formula or breast milk. The milk will continue to balance out baby's nutritional needs, though, so do not replace it with whole milk until the child is at least one year old. Whole cow's milk contains too much protein and fat for the young digestive system.

BRING ON THE FOOD

Once your baby accepts cereals, she will be ready for vegetables and fruits. Always introduce only one food at a time; this way you can make sure your child does not have an allergic reaction. Then, wait five to seven days before going on to a new food. Carrots are an easy vegetable to start with. When serving them for the first time, purée the cooked vegetable until completely smooth. If lumps remain, strain the vegetable through a fine mesh sieve. Add a few tablespoons of formula or breast milk, a taste with which your baby is familiar. Once your baby has accepted the carrots, or any new food, you can mix it with plain water instead, to make a smooth purée.

After your baby is used to several different fruits and vegetables, begin to combine them. Recipes like Green Bean Purée with Pear, Caramelized Onions with Apples and Carrots, or Sweet Potatoes with Peaches are included in this chapter. The whole family will love them as chunky side dishes and baby will enjoy them as blended purées.

Once your child is looking forward to solid food, introduce her to some that are high in protein, such as puréed meat, chicken, fish, and cottage cheese, and eggs, and yogurt.

By nine months, your child will be able to swallow food with the occasional small lump. Pieces of bread, cooked vegetables, peeled, soft fruit wedges, tender bites of meat, and small chunks of soft cheese add variety to a diet of purées. Cut soft-cooked vegetables (such as green beans) into ⅛-inch pieces and scatter them around her tray; this way the baby can feed herself with her hands while you are warming the rest of the meal.

By seven to ten months, your baby should be eating three meals daily, plus snacks, and drinking less milk since she gets more nourishment from solid foods. Still, even by one year of age, most of your baby's nutrients will come from breast milk or formula.

WHAT'S TO DRINK?

Breast milk or formula is your baby's primary nourishing fluid. Two to 3½ cups a day are adequate for most healthy babies. Too much at this point in a baby's diet can displace other foods necessary to provide certain nutrients, especially iron. Remember, when your baby starts drinking cow's milk, it should be whole milk since babies need the fats in whole milk.

When you introduce fruits, you may also introduce diluted fruit juice at the same time. Use one part juice to three parts water to start. Even if you don't give your infant juice, do be sure to give her lots of water between feedings. Babies lose more water through the kidneys and skin than adults, and are prone to losing water through vomiting and diarrhea. As a rule of thumb, allow ¼ ounce of water for each pound of body weight each day.

DON'T SHAKE THE SALT

Remember, there is no need to salt your baby's food, even if your taste buds demand salt. Get out of the salt habit and use spices and herbs to flavor food instead. Our recipes make lots of suggestions. Babies don't know the difference between salted and unsalted food, so encourage good habits from the start. Most canned vegetables are loaded with salt; use fresh or unsalted frozen vegetables for the whole family.

TOO MUCH OF A GOOD THING!

Fat babies were once considered healthy babies. Some people still believe that, but the truth is that fat babies are likely to grow into obese adults. As we've mentioned before, feed your baby well, but don't overfeed! A one-year-old, twenty-pound infant needs about 900 to 1,000 calories a day. This can easily be gotten from three cups of whole milk, an egg, and a few tablespoons each of cottage cheese, cereal, strained fruit, and vegetables with some chopped meat. Some babies will need more, some less. If your baby is overweight, don't underfeed. He still needs the nutrients in wholesome food. Increase his activity and make sure every calorie counts.

At-a-Glance Schedule

As the chart below shows, your baby will move quickly from strained foods that are almost liquids to solid chopped ones.

5 to 6 Months

Strained foods	Iron-fortified cereals, soft-cooked vegetables and fruits puréed, then strained to a smooth consistency

6 to 8 Months

Puréed foods	Cooked fruits and vegetables puréed to a smooth consistency, fruit juices mixed with water

8 to 10 Months

Finely minced or coarsely puréed foods	Small finger foods (macaroni, bits of potato, rice), soft-cooked pieces of vegetable, raw ripe fruits

10 to 12 Months

Chopped foods	Small pieces of meat, cheese, and hard-cooked eggs

BABY'S ON THE ROAD

Depending on how you look at it, six to twelve months can be either the easiest or the hardest age to travel with. You don't need a lot of toys, but the hungries attack your child often. Even at the ripe age of six months, babies still need to be held while you are feeding them. This will require stopping along the way, which can be annoying. Don't try to stretch out an extra mile; just give yourself plenty of time.

STEAMED CARROTS

C arrots are a wonderful introduction to solid food. The smaller, thinner carrots are sweetest.

PREPARATION TIME: 10 minutes
COOKING TIME: 7 to 10 minutes
FREEZES: 2 months

5 thin carrots, peeled, trimmed, and sliced ½ inch thick

1. Bring 1 inch water in a medium saucepan to a boil. Place the carrots in a steaming basket and set the basket in the pan. Lower the heat, cover the pan, and steam until the carrots are tender, 7 to 10 minutes.

2. Transfer the carrots to a blender or food processor and process to the desired consistency. Add water 1 teaspoon at a time, if needed, to make a smoother purée. Freeze any purée that you are not using right away.

MAKES 1¾ CUPS

BAKED SWEET POTATOES

A sweet potato is one of nature's sweetest confections. Children also love its bright orange color.

PREPARATION TIME: 5 minutes
COOKING TIME: 1 hour (baked); 10 minutes (steamed)
FREEZES: 2 months

3 medium sweet potatoes

1. Preheat the oven to 350°F.

2. Scrub the potatoes under running water and

pat dry. Prick each potato several times with a fork. Bake the potatoes until tender when pierced with a fork, about 1 hour. Cut the potatoes in half and scoop the pulp out of the skins.

Note: For the very young child, process the potatoes in a blender or food processor, adding water, 1 teaspoon at a time, to the desired consistency. If cooking the potatoes for a toddler, just mash them a bit with a fork. Freeze any purée that you are not using right away.

MAKES 2 CUPS

SWEET POTATOES WITH PEACHES

Try serving plain baked or steamed sweet potatoes to your young eater first. Once you are sure she enjoys the taste, blend it with ripe peaches or other favorite fresh fruits.

PREPARATION TIME: 10 minutes
COOKING TIME: 12 to 15 minutes
FREEZES: 2 months

*3 medium sweet potatoes, peeled and cut into
  1/2-inch-thick slices*
*2 ripe medium peaches, peeled, pitted, and cut
  into wedges*

1. Bring 1 inch water in a medium saucepan to a boil. Place the potatoes in a steaming basket and set the basket in the pan. Lower the heat, cover the pan, and steam 6 minutes. Add the peaches to the basket, cover again, and steam until the potatoes are tender, 4 minutes longer.

2. Transfer the potatoes and peaches to a blender or food processor. Process to the desired consistency, adding water, 1 teaspoon at a time, if needed. Freeze any purée that you are not using right away.

MAKES 2½ CUPS

BAKED ACORN SQUASH

Too often we think to prepare acorn squash only when autumn leaves are changing their colors and the squash are left lying in dry fields. A hardy vegetable, it can usually be found all year long and is easy to prepare.

PREPARATION TIME: 5 minutes
COOKING TIME: 1 hour
FREEZES: 2 months

2 small acorn squash
2 tablespoons frozen apple juice concentrate,
thawed
¼ teaspoon cinnamon (optional)

1. Preheat the oven to 375°F.

2. Cut each squash in half and scoop out the seeds. Divide the juice concentrate and cinnamon among the 4 halves and cover with aluminum foil. Place the squash in a baking pan. Bake until tender when pierced with a fork, about 1 hour.

3. Remove the foil and let the squash cool for a few minutes. Scrape the meat from one half and purée it in a blender or food processor for the smallest family member. Freeze any purée that you are not using right away.

MAKES 2 CUPS

STEAMED BUTTERNUT SQUASH WITH GRAPES

Once your child is eating plain steamed butternut squash, add puréed grapes for a more interesting flavor.

PREPARATION TIME: 10 minutes
COOKING TIME: 12 minutes
FREEZES: 2 months

1 medium butternut squash (1¼ pounds),
peeled, seeded and cut into 1-inch cubes
(2½ cups)
18 seedless green grapes, rinsed and stemmed

1. Bring 1 inch water in a medium saucepan to a boil. Place the squash in a steaming basket and set the basket in the pan. Lower the heat, cover the pan, and steam for 6 minutes. Add the grapes to the basket, cover again, and steam until the squash is very soft and tender, about 6 minutes longer.

2. Transfer the grapes and squash to a blender or food processor and process to the consistency you want. Add 1 teaspoon water if you want a thinner and smoother purée. Freeze any purée that you are not using right away.

MAKES 2½ CUPS

GREEN BEANS WITH PEARS

After introducing your child to plain string beans, try him out on this combination. Then add a sprinkling of ground cardamom or cinnamon, a tiny pinch of crumbled rosemary, or a little apple juice concentrate for a change of pace. Older family members will enjoy this served as a chunky side dish.

PREPARATION TIME: 10 minutes
COOKING TIME: 6 minutes
FREEZES: 2 months

¾ pound fresh green beans, trimmed and cut
*   into 2-inch pieces*
2 pears, quartered, peeled, and cored

1. Bring 1 inch water in a medium saucepan to a boil. Place the green beans and pears in a steaming basket and set the basket in the pan. Lower the heat, cover the pan, and steam until the beans are tender, about 6 minutes.

2. Transfer the beans and pears to a blender or food processor and process for 1 minute. If you want a smoother purée, add water, 1 teaspoon

A Reminder

When starting your infant on solid foods, strain purées to get the smoothest consistency possible.

at a time, until you have the consistency that you want. Freeze any purée that you are not using right away.

MAKES 2 CUPS

STEAMED ASPARAGUS

Asparagus is one of the wonders of spring. Many cooks consider thick asparagus inferior to the thinner stalks because they generally have woodier bases. The problem can be handled easily with the swish of a paring knife.

PREPARATION TIME: 10 minutes
COOKING TIME: 7 to 9 minutes
FREEZES: 2 months

1 pound fresh asparagus

1. Trim the woody bottoms from the asparagus, then peel the stalks, using a vegetable peeler. Cut the asparagus into 3-inch lengths and place in a steaming basket.

2. Bring 1 inch water in a medium saucepan to a boil. Lower the heat, set the steaming basket in the pan, and cover. Steam until the asparagus is tender, 7 to 9 minutes.

3. Transfer the asparagus to a blender or food processor and process to the consistency you want. Add water, 1 teaspoon at a time, if needed, to make a smoother purée. Freeze any purée that you are not using right away.

MAKES 2½ CUPS

STEAMED GREEN PEA PUREE

Fresh peas are delicious, but they can be unpredictable. If left a little too long on the vine, they become tough and a bit bitter, which of course is reflected in the finished purée. Buy early peas, tender and fresh; otherwise, you can substitute frozen peas. Peas play well with additional flavors from herbs and seasonings. Try them with a few freshly cut ribbons of mint—a taste the older kids will ask for again!

PREPARATION TIME: 5 to 8 minutes
COOKING TIME: 7 to 10 minutes
FREEZES: 2 months

¾ pound fresh peas, shelled (1 cup), or 1 package (10 ounces; 2½ cups) frozen peas

1. Bring 1 inch water in a medium saucepan to a boil. Place the peas in a steaming basket and set the basket in the pan. Lower the heat, cover the pan, and steam until the peas are tender, about 7 minutes fresh peas, 6 minutes frozen. The steaming time will, of course, vary with the freshness of the peas.

2. Transfer the peas to a blender or food processor and process to the consistency you want. Add water, 1 teaspoon at a time, if needed, to make a smoother purée. Freeze any purée that you are not using right away.

MAKES 1 CUP PUREE FROM FRESH PEAS, 1¾ CUPS PUREE FROM FROZEN PEAS

STEAMED BEETS WITH CUCUMBER AND MINT

Although it's great fun to mix and match new tastes and flavors with puréed foods, remember to introduce new foods slowly and check for reactions. Once you have a green light, food combinations have no limits. Don't purée the adults' portions. This makes an elegant, refreshing side dish to steamed fish.

PREPARATION TIME: 15 minutes
COOKING TIME: 14 minutes
FREEZES: 2 months

4 or 5 medium (2 inch) beets, peeled, roots trimmed, and sliced ¼ inch thick
2 medium cucumbers, peeled, seeded, and coarsely chopped
5 fresh mint leaves, thinly sliced

1. Bring 1 inch water in a medium saucepan to a boil. Place the beet slices in a steaming basket and set the basket in the pan. Lower the heat, cover the pan, and steam until the beets are tender, about 10 minutes. Add the cucumbers and mint to the beets and steam 3 minutes longer.

2. Transfer the vegetables to a blender or food processor and process to the consistency you want. Add water, 1 teaspoon at a time, if needed to make a smoother purée. Freeze any purée that you are not using right away.

MAKES 2 CUPS

CAUTION FOODS

As explained in Chapter One, small pieces of foods can present a choking problem for young children. Do not serve any of the following "caution foods" unless they are mashed, puréed, or strained: nuts, olives, popcorn, sunflower seeds, peas, corn kernels, hot dog slices, chips, pieces of raw carrot or other hard vegetable, grapes, cherries, and raisins.

Also remember the warning about honey: It can cause severe food poisoning in children under one year.

STEWED TOMATOES WITH APPLES

Sugar is often added to the tomatoes to insure that the dish has a sweet taste. You won't need to add sugar if you cook them with fresh apples or even with apple juice concentrate. This delicious variation can be puréed for the tiny tot and left chunky for older children. Once your child starts eating meats, you'll find this makes a great mix with chicken, beef, or cooked dried beans.

PREPARATION TIME: 15 to 20 minutes
COOKING TIME: 8 minutes
FREEZES: 2 months

3 ripe medium tomatoes
2 McIntosh apples, peeled, cored, and quartered

1. Bring a pot of water to a boil. Cut the cores from the tomatoes, then cut an X through just the skin on the bottom of each. Drop the tomatoes in the boiling water for about 30 seconds, or a little longer if the tomatoes are less than ripe. Immediately transfer the tomatoes to a bowl of cold water. When they have cooled, peel them. The skins should slip off easily.

2. Cut each tomato in half and squeeze out the seeds. Roughly chop the tomatoes. Place the tomatoes and apples in a small saucepan. Cook, covered over medium heat until the apples are tender, about 8 minutes.

3. Transfer the tomatoes and apples to a blender or food processor. Process to the consistency you want. Freeze any purée that you are not using right away.

MAKES 2 CUPS

STEAMED SPINACH WITH PEARS

S pinach with pears is simple, and the flavors complement each other deliciously.

PREPARATION TIME: 7 minutes
COOKING TIME: 6 minutes
FREEZES: 2 months

¾ pound fresh spinach, thoroughly rinsed and stems removed
2 ripe pears, peeled, cored, and coarsely chopped

1. Rinse the spinach leaves one last time, shake off the excess water, and place leaves in a heavy medium saucepan. Add the pears, cover, and steam over medium-high heat for 6 minutes.

2. Transfer the pears and spinach to a blender or food processor. Process 1 minute, adding 1 teaspoon of water, if needed, to make the purée smoother or thinner. Freeze any purée that you are not using right away.

MAKES 1½ CUPS

STEAMED APPLESAUCE

K eep plenty of this sauce on hand. You'll find it will become a staple in your freezer. Some tasty additions to this fruit purée are ground nutmeg or cinnamon and other puréed fruits such as bananas, pears, apricots, or plums.

PREPARATION TIME: 15 minutes
COOKING TIME: 6 minutes
FREEZES: 2 months

6 medium apples (McIntosh or Rome Beauties), peeled, cored, and thickly sliced

1. Bring 1 inch water in a large saucepan to a boil. Place the apple slices in a steaming basket large enough to hold them comfortably, and set the basket in the pan. Lower the heat, cover the pan, and steam until the apples are tender, about 6 minutes.

2. Transfer the apples to a blender or food processor and process to the consistency you want. Freeze any purée that you are not using right away.

MAKES 3 CUPS

CARAMELIZED ONIONS WITH APPLES AND CARROTS

One of the little-known secrets about onions is that when they are cooked *slowly* in a small amount of oil, their bitterness goes away and a wonderful, natural sweetness remains. The mouth-watering combination of caramelized onions, tangy apples, and sweet carrots is one that you and your children will enjoy long after your baby has grown.

PREPARATION TIME: 20 minutes
COOKING TIME: 25 minutes
FREEZES: 2 months

1 teaspoon safflower oil
1 medium onion, peeled and thinly sliced
1 apple, peeled, cored, and thinly sliced
2 carrots, peeled, trimmed, and thinly sliced
¼ cup water

1. Place the oil and onions in a medium skillet. Cook slowly, stirring occasionally, over medium-low heat until brown, about 15 minutes.

2. Add the apples, carrots, and water. Cover and continue to cook slowly until the carrots are tender, 5 to 7 minutes.

3. Purée some of the onion mixture in a blender or food processor for your baby. Serve the rest as it is to your family. Freeze any purée that you are not using right away.

MAKES 2 CUPS

APRICOT AND PEAR PUREE

You haven't experienced great taste until you have eaten a fresh apricot. The apricot season is a short one, so when you see them, grab them. Teach your baby what exquisite flavor really is!

PREPARATION TIME: 10 minutes
COOKING TIME: 6 minutes
FREEZES: 2 months

2 ripe pears, peeled, cored, and sliced
5 fresh apricots, halved and pitted

1. Bring 1 inch water in a medium saucepan to a boil. Place the fruits in a steaming basket and set the basket in the pan. Lower the heat, cover the pan, and steam until the pears are tender, about 6 minutes.

2. Remove the steaming basket from the pan,

SWEETENING FRUIT

Fruit that is well ripened is naturally sweet. Before serving a fruit purée to your baby, take a taste. If it seems tart, add ½ to 1 teaspoon of thawed apple juice concentrate to sweeten.

and let the fruit stand until cool enough to handle. Peel the apricots.

3. Place the fruits in a blender or food processor and process 1 minute. If you want a smoother purée, add water, 1 teaspoon at a time, until the purée is the consistency you want. Freeze any purée that you are not using right away.

MAKES 1½ CUPS

SWEET PEACH PUREE

Peaches, like most fruits, can be puréed either cooked or raw. For the child younger than eight months, it is better to soften the fruit a bit with either a quick steaming or a toss in a pan with a tablespoon of water over medium heat. When the fruit is puréed, it will be smoother and easier to eat.

PREPARATION TIME: 15 minutes
COOKING TIME: 5 minutes
FREEZES: 2 months

4 medium peaches

1. Bring a medium saucepan of water to a boil. Cut a shallow X in the skin of each peach. Drop the peaches into the boiling water and blanch them for 1 minute. (Leave them in a little longer if they are not quite ripe.)

2. Quickly cool the peaches in a bowl of cold water. Slip off the skins. Cut peach in half and remove the pits. Slice the halves ½-inch thick.

3. Bring 1 inch water in a medium saucepan to a boil. Place the fruit in a steaming basket and set the basket in the pan. Lower the heat, cover the pan, and steam until the peaches are tender, about 5 minutes.

4. Transfer the fruit to a blender or food processor and process to the consistency you want. Freeze any purée that you are not using right away.

MAKES 2 CUPS

WARM PLUM PUREE

A ripe plum will satisfy almost any sweet tooth. Select those that are soft, but un-bruised. When plums are ripe, the skins peel away easily with a paring knife. Blanching the fruit in boiling water before peeling will encourage any hard-to-peel fruit.

Plums do not necessarily need to be cooked before puréeing. You may find it necessary only when your child is just beginning to eat solid foods. Cooking less is best!

PREPARATION TIME: 10 minutes
COOKING TIME: 5 minutes
FREEZES: 2 months

6 medium plums, peeled, halved, and pitted

1. If you are making the purée for a young baby, soften the plums by simmering them with 2 tablespoons water over medium-high heat until tender, about 4 minutes.

THINNING PURÉES

When you first introduce your baby to solid foods, thin out the consistency with a taste she can recognize such as breast milk or formula. Gradually reduce the amount of liquid as your baby learns to swallow solids and enjoy them. Later on, some purées naturally will be very thick. At this time you may want to thin it with water, juice, formula, or breast milk.

2. Place the fruit (cooked or raw) in a blender or food processor and process for 1 minute. Freeze any purée that you are not using right away.

MAKES 1½ CUPS

SPRING STRAWBERRY PUREE

You know it's spring when strawberries find their way to your local market.

Take advantage of strawberry season by putting some away in the freezer for berry-less months. Hull them and freeze on a baking sheet. When the berries are frozen, remove them from the sheet and seal in a plastic bag.

PREPARATION TIME: 10 minutes
COOKING TIME: 3 minutes (for new eaters only)
FREEZES: 2 months

1 pint strawberries

1. Rinse the berries well and hull them just before puréeing them. If your child is just beginning to eat solid foods, first cook the berries with 1 tablespoon water briefly over medium heat. Place the berries in a food processor or blender and process to the desired consistency.

2. Serve the purée as is or mix it with other fruits, vegetables, or meats. You may want to strain out the tiny strawberry seeds for the new eater. Freeze any purée that you are not using right away.

MAKES 1¼ CUPS

STRAWBERRIES WITH BANANA AND MINT

Bananas taste great by themselves, but they also combine well with other fruit. One all-time favorite combination is strawberries with banana and mint.

PREPARATION TIME: 10 minutes
FREEZES: 2 months

2 cups strawberries, rinsed and hulled
1 banana, peeled and cut into chunks
8 mint leaves, cut into thin strips

1 teaspoon frozen apple juice concentrate, thawed

1. Place the strawberries, banana, and mint in a food processor or blender and process to the desired consistency.

2. Add the juice concentrate and process just to blend. Freeze any purée you are not using right away.

MAKES 2 CUPS

SNAZZY FRITTATAS

You can begin to feed your child whole eggs by the end of the tenth month, because your baby will be able to digest egg whites as well as yolks. A frittata is a baked omelet and is a great way to turn a little leftover vegetable purée into another dish.

PREPARATION TIME: 10 minutes
COOKING TIME: 45 minutes
REFRIGERATES: 2 days
FREEZES: 1 month

1½ teaspoons safflower oil for brushing around the pan
4 large eggs
¼ cup vegetable purée (see pages 35–43)
3 leaves fresh basil cut into thin strips

1. Preheat the oven to 325°F. Brush a 6-inch ovenproof skillet or pan with the oil.

2. Whisk the eggs, vegetable purée, and basil together. Pour it into the oiled skillet and bake until the eggs are firm; about 45 minutes.

3. Remove the skillet from the oven and let it cool slightly. Cut the frittata into wedges for your family and tiny bite-size pieces for your child.

MAKES ONE 6-INCH FRITTATA

YOGURT

Yogurt is a staple for young children, so why not serve them the freshest possible? An additional bonus: homemade yogurt is fortified with vitamin A; commercial yogurt is not. Remember, children under two need their yogurt made with whole milk.

Once you've made your first batch, reserve enough to start the next.

PREPARATION TIME: 8 hours
REFRIGERATES: 5 days

1 quart whole milk
4 tablespoons (¼ cup) active-culture plain yogurt

1. Warm the milk in a saucepan to 180°F, then let cool to 110°F.

2. Stir in the yogurt, about 1 tablespoon for each cup of milk. Let stand in a warm spot (106° to 108°F) for 8 hours. A gas oven warmed by a pilot light might be just right. (Also, there are yogurt-making gadgets available today that keep the yogurt at the correct temperature for culturing in individual containers—a foolproof method and so cheap.)

3. Refrigerate the finished yogurt.

MAKES 1 QUART

FRUITED YOGURT

Commercial fruit yogurts are made with unnecessary sugar. It is easy and healthier to make your own.

PREPARATION TIME: 15 minutes
REFRIGERATES: 1 day

⅓ cup mixed ripe fruit (washed, hulled berries; peeled, pitted peaches; bananas)
2 teaspoons frozen apple juice concentrate, thawed
½ teaspoon vanilla or almond extract
⅓ cup plain yogurt, preferably homemade

1. Chop the fruit into small chunks. (For very young eaters, purée the chunks in a blender or food processor.)

2. Add the fruit and flavorings to the yogurt and stir to combine.

3. Serve immediately or cover and store in the refrigerator.

SERVES 2 YOUNG CHILDREN

BARLEY SOUP

Barley cereals are among the first foods most people give their children. As your child develops, you can take barley a step further with this savory soup. Purée baby's portion; leave it chunky for the rest of the family. For a young

baby, substitute water for the broth.

PREPARATION TIME: 20 minutes
COOKING TIME: 1½ hours
FREEZES: 2 months

½ cup plus 2 tablespoons barley
5 cups salt-free chicken, beef, or vegetable broth
  (preferably homemade), or more if needed
1 carrot, peeled, trimmed, and cut into 2-inch
  pieces
1 small onion, studded with 4 cloves
1 bay leaf

1. Place barley, 4 cups of the broth, the carrot, onion, and bay leaf in a large saucepan and bring to a boil over medium-high heat. Reduce the heat and let simmer uncovered until the barley is soft, about 1½ hours. Stir occasionally

and check from time to time that there is enough liquid. Add additional broth 1 cup at a time, as needed.

2. Remove the onion with cloves and the bay leaf. Measure out the amount you want for your baby and process it in a blender or food processor, about 1 minute.

3. Serve the remaining soup to your family with a salad and some good, crusty bread.

MAKES ABOUT 1 QUART

YELLOW OR GREEN SPLIT PEA SOUP

T he trusty split pea has long been a staple in the family cupboard. It is not only tasty; it's a great source of protein, especially useful before you have introduced meats to your baby.

PREPARATION TIME: 20 minutes
COOKING TIME: 1 hour
FREEZES: 2 months

1 pound yellow or green split peas, rinsed thoroughly and picked over
1½ quarts salt-free beef, chicken, or vegetable broth (preferably homemade), or more if needed
1 carrot, peeled, trimmed, and cut into ½-inch pieces

1 rib celery, trimmed and cut into ½-inch pieces
1 onion, sliced
1 bay leaf

1. Place all the ingredients in a large saucepan and bring to a boil over medium-high heat. Reduce the heat and simmer uncovered until the split peas are very soft, about 1 hour. Check from time to time that there's enough liquid. Add stock, 1 cup at a time, as needed.

2. Purée the soup you want to serve your baby. Serve the remaining soup with a green salad and crusty loaf of bread.

MAKES ABOUT 1½ QUARTS

CHAPTER THREE

Your Child from 12 to 18 Months

A child's first birthday certainly is a landmark event. Within that span of time, you have watched enthusiastically as your baby hits all the early milestones, from first smiles to first steps. But, he has been hitting milestones in less visible ways, too.

To begin with, your infant's body could digest only breast milk or formula, then was able to handle cereals, then puréed fruits, all within a relatively short period of time. Now, at twelve months, your baby is ready to enjoy many varieties of foods, and dishes prepared fresh by you are far richer in flavors than any that are jarred or dried. But, in your enthusiasm to feed your child well, do remember not to bombard poor baby with many new dishes all at once! Remember, too, to introduce new foods one at a time and watch for allergic reactions. Recipes in this book for 12- to 18-month-old babies include familiar foods along with exciting new ones.

WELCOME TO THE TABLE, BABY!

Adapting food for the year-old baby is really quite easy. All you'll need are a knife and fork. Foods that are cooked soft, such as stews or steamed vegetables, can be mashed with a fork. Firmer foods, such as braised or roasted meats, should be cut into pieces ¼ inch or less (remember that your child at 12 months will probably have only two to four front teeth). If the meat is too tough to be eaten even in small bits, process it briefly in a blender or food processor to break it down.

You may notice that your baby's appetite decreases around his first birthday. This is because a baby's growth rate naturally slows down after the first year. The quantities of food he consumes on any given day may fluctuate from positively gargantuan to seemingly miniscule amounts. Be assured that healthy children will not intentionally go hungry or stuff themselves needlessly! Children's eating habits are established in these formative years; do your baby, your family, and yourself a favor by setting a good example. Never force your baby to finish a meal, as this could spell trouble later on in the form of a weight problem. Eat a variety of nu-

tritious foods, take your time eating them, and enjoy your food. Don't keep a lot of sugary foods around to tempt the family, and never use dessert as a reward. Remember, now that your child is 12 months old, he can drink whole cow's milk. As we've explained before, children under two shouldn't have low-fat or skim milk.

A meal at the family dinner table can be either a riotous calamity or a relaxed hour of togetherness. Your own attitudes as a parent about mealtime and your response to your baby's table behavior will set the stage. Babies at this age experiment. Watching yours dump plate after plate on the floor as an expression of independence can wear thin after a while; still don't feel it's a disaster if your child plays with mashed potatoes or uses his fingers to eat peas. Let your baby enjoy the food experience, even if it means a bit more of a mess for you. Children 12 to 18 months take great delight in feeding themselves, but their aim with a spoon is not always right on target. It's a good idea to have plenty of finger foods around.

Your one-year-old will probably be eating three meals plus snacks. It is important to offer food at regular intervals. Don't let your child wait more than several hours before offering him something to eat.

BALANCED DIETS

To insure that your child develops a diet based on the Four Basic Food Groups, offer her a variety of foods each day. Understand, however, that she may not always eat "balanced" meals. Encourage, do not force. If foods from the different groups are available, children will eventually balance their own diets. Remember, in the early years, a serving size is generally measured as one tablespoon per year of life.

Bread, Cereal, and Starchy Vegetable Group: 4 Servings. The breads and cereals you give your child should be whole-grain or enriched to provide B vitamins and iron. Among the many choices are favorites like whole-wheat bread, oatmeal, unsweetened dry cereal, pasta, brown rice, and barley. Starchy vegetables, such as potatoes, corn, and winter squash, are included in this group as well. The vitamins, minerals, and fiber in these high-carbohydrate foods are important to your child's nutrition.

Fruit and Vegetable Group: 4 servings. These foods are high in carbohydrates and contribute fiber, vitamins A, C, and E, as well as important minerals such as potassium, magnesium, calcium, and some iron. Try to include a good source of vitamin C (citrus fruit, strawberries, broccoli, tomatoes) and a good source of vitamin A (cantaloupe, tomato, winter squash, sweet potato, broccoli) every day. Don't worry if your child won't eat green vegetables. Offer a variety of fruits and non-green vegetables (carrots, squash, sweet potatoes). Chances are slim that your child will become malnourished because he or she does not eat green vegetables for a period of time! For a child 12 to 18 months, a serving is 2 tablespoons or less of sliced fruit or vegetables.

Dairy Group: 2 to 3 cups of milk, or equivalent. Use regular whole milk and dairy products unless your pediatrician advises otherwise. This group provides a good source of protein and vitamin D, provided your child drinks vitamin D-fortified milk. It is also the best source of calcium, an important mineral needed for proper growth and bone formation. One cup of plain yogurt contains the same amount of calcium found in 1 cup of milk, so substitute one for the other. However, this does not hold true for all dairy products. You would have to eat 2 cups of cottage cheese to get the calcium equivalent found in 1 cup of milk.

Meat and Meat Alternatives Group: 2 Servings. These foods provide the major sources of protein. The best sources are lean meat, poultry, fish, eggs, and legumes (dry peas and beans). However, none of us needs large portions of red meat to satisfy protein requirements. In fact, an 18-month-old girl weighing 25 pounds could satisfy her daily protein needs by eating 1 ounce of chicken, 1 tablespoon of peanut butter, and ¼ cup of cottage cheese.

Most toddlers, even confirmed meathaters, who eat a varied diet will get the protein they need to thrive. A child one to three years of age needs about 23 grams of protein daily. She can get it simply by having 1 cup of milk (8 grams), an egg (6 grams), 1 ounce of cheese (7 grams), and 1 slice of bread (2 grams). As long as the child eats 2 servings of protein foods a day, there should be no problem with inadequate intake.

This group also provides the best sources of the dietary iron (found especially in red meat and liver) needed for healthy blood and muscles.

Young children need 15 milligrams of iron per day, almost as much as an adult female (18 milligrams). The peak prevalence of iron-deficiency anemia is at approximately 18 months. If your child's diet is composed largely of milk and other foods with a low iron content, iron deficiency might be a concern.

VITAMIN AND MINERAL SUPPLEMENTS

Assuming your toddler is healthy and receiving a normal diet, there is no need for vitamin and mineral supplements. Never give your child supplements except under your pediatrician's direction.

OUR RECIPES

Let's take a quick look at one of our recipes and see how it stacks up against the Four Basic. Red Bean Pie is a meal in itself and provides plenty of nutrients for your child, as well as for your whole family. Here's the low-down on its high nutrition: the beef and beans provide protein and iron. The beans and cornmeal contribute carbohydrate clout in the form of fiber, and also iron. The vegetables (tomatoes and bell peppers) add vitamins A and C, potassium, and magnesium. The milk and cheese have lots of calcium. We have covered all four groups.

A WORD ABOUT FATS

Moderate amounts of oil, butter, or margarine may be used to prepare and flavor food, but excessive use of fats contributes to weight problems. Too much saturated fat (found in butter, animal fat, and hydrogenated oils) increases the risk for heart disease. Don't restrict fat in your toddler's diet too much, but don't go overboard and drown everything in butter, oil, or cream. Our recipes contain little added fat, so they are "heart healthy."

HOW SWEET IT IS: THE SUGAR STORY

The preference for a sweet taste appears to be inborn in most infants. How strong an attraction sweets hold for them is based in part on influences such as parents' and siblings' sweet habits, television advertising, peer pressure, and experience. If you want your child to show restraint and moderation, you must set a good example in your approach to refined sweets and desserts. Always have fresh fruit available. Offer it in a tasty and appealing fashion. Homemade cookies and muffins can be made nutritious by limiting fat and sugar, using natural sweeteners such as apple juice concentrate, mashed bananas, or raisins.

BREAKFAST: OFF TO A GOOD START

We all know how important a nourishing breakfast is; it sustains us through the morning hours. Your baby needs that nourishment, too. But not everyone is ready to eat first thing. If he refuses food, try again a little later on. Don't let your child wait until lunch time before having his first food of the day. Again, let your tod-

> ## PORTION SIZES
>
> Because the recipes in this book are designed to feed families, not just babies, each lists the number of portions it will make in adult amounts. Remember, the amounts younger children eat will vary. A good starting point for every meal is to offer 1 tablespoon of each food for each year of life.

dler experiment feeding himself. If he enjoys breakfast, he is more likely to eat it.

SMART SNACKING

Snacks are an important way to supplement Baby's nutrition. Finger foods such as chunks of soft fruits and vegetables with dip, cheeses, or nut spreads on whole grain crackers are easy to prepare and are loved by children of all ages. Don't offer your toddler chips, candy, or soda. There's little nutritional value there, and you may find you have a cookie monster on your hands if you're not cautious about sugary snacks. Try Peanut 'n' Jam Squares (see Index) for a sweet treat! When your child asks for food, determine whether he is simply thirsty or truly hungry. Serve water, diluted fruit juices or a Kid Fizz made with seltzer water and fruit juice. If you feel that snacks are spoiling your child's appetite for meals, reduce the snacks or give only water or juice. You may want to change

slightly the hours at which you serve meals, depending on your child's hunger, but you don't need to rearrange the whole family's schedule to accommodate your one-year-old.

FOOD FIXATIONS

Food likes and dislikes in young children come and go. Their whims may dictate only mashed potatoes one day, and only milk the next. Your child may suddenly hate vegetables, especially the green ones. It is usually temporary. Serve the vegetables your child does seem to enjoy and occasionally "test" the ones which have been refused before. You can even sneak puréed vegetables into soup, meat loaf, or spaghetti sauce. Be sure you offer your "veggie hater" lots of fresh or unsweetened fruit, which contains many of the same vitamins and minerals found in vegetables. If you make the foods available, most healthy young children will get the nutrients they need over the course of a week or so. If your child continues on an extremely limited selection of foods for weeks on end, consult your pediatrician.

OVERWEIGHT ISN'T HEALTHY

As we've said before, by feeding your child properly from the beginning, you will avoid this problem altogether. But, if your toddler is overweight, get her on the road to good eating as soon as you become aware of the problem. Use common sense and don't serve your child puddings, creamed soups or vegetables, cake, candy, cookies, or ice cream. Encourage your child to be active—jumping, tumbling, and walking—and don't let her spend the entire day in a crib or playpen or in front of the television.

APPETIZING LUNCHES

When trying to get a baby ready for nursery or playcare by 8:00 AM, it certainly is tempting for working parents to send along a jarred lunch. Instead, take advantage of leftovers; cut into tiny pieces or mashed, they can make a great lunch. If dinner's all gone, there are many other ways lunch to prepare on the run. Here are a few ideas:

- Pita wedges stuffed with tuna, soft-cooked bits of green beans, and yogurt with banana pieces
- Zucchini Pizza Strips (cut into small bits), a bagel, and milk
- Stuffed pasta shells with vegetable purée and cottage cheese, pear cubes with grated cheddar, and Granola Squares

STROLLING FOODS

It seems that babies are always hungry when you are out for a walk or running errands. Just because you are away from home is no reason to be thoughtless about what you give your child to eat. There are plenty of quick nutritious snacks available, store-bought or homemade. No matter how tired you are or how desperately you want to satisfy your child quickly, don't fall back on the empty calories of sugary treats. Make sure all the foods you give your child count. With that in mind, keep on hand: rice cakes, bagels, salt-free whole wheat pretzels, pieces of fruit, Cheerios, small juice boxes or bottles, cheese cubes, and pre-made sandwiches (or sandwich filling, minced into bits). Be sure to pack a selection each time the two of you leave home.

CAUTION FOODS

It is important to remember to keep nuts, olives, popcorn, sunflower seeds, peas, corn kernels, hot dog slices, chips, pieces of raw carrot or other hard vegetables, grapes, cherries, and raisins away from your child unless they are mashed, chopped, or finely ground.

Your 12-month-old can now have honey without any problem.

THE SYMBOLS

At the end of each recipe, we have marked which of the Four Basic Food groups are contained in that recipe. Most supply your child with more than one.

Bread, Cereal, and Starchy Vegetables:

Fruit and Vegetables:

Dairy:

Meat and Meat Alternatives:

WEEKLY MENU SUGGESTIONS: 12 to 18 MONTHS

	Breakfast	Snack
SUNDAY	Fruited Yogurt; Apple juice	Bagel Milk
MONDAY	Fresh fruit shakes Sliced whole-grain bread	Yogurt with mashed bananas
TUESDAY	Unsugared breakfast cereal with fruit and milk	Fruit muffin Apple juice
WEDNESDAY	Poached egg with toast Apple juice	Peach Purée with cottage cheese
THURSDAY	Pear Salad with Yogurt and Cheese Bran muffin; Juice	Flaked tuna and apple pieces
FRIDAY	Broiled open-face cheese sandwich Orange juice	Cottage cheese with strawberries
SATURDAY	Banana Pancakes with Peach Purée; Milk	Peanut butter on bread slices; Milk

Lunch	Snack	Dinner
Omelet or scrambled egg with cooked vegetable bits and grated cheese; Juice	Peeled, sliced peach	Orangy Baked Chicken Nutted Rice Pilaf Squashed Squash; Milk
Orangy Baked Chicken bits Peeled cucumber pieces High Tide Seashells; Milk	Bagel or bran muffin Juice	Eggplant and Cheese Stacks Mashed steamed peas and carrots with dill Green salad; Bread; Milk
Garden Gazpacho Whole-grained bread Cheese cubes; Milk	Pear halves with yogurt and grated cheese	Hearty Fish Chowder Green bean salad Apple Snow
Hearty Fish Chowder and green bean bits; Juice	Apple and banana pieces	Red Bean Pie Soft cooked carrots Milk
Zucchini Pizza Strips Bagel or slice bread; Milk	Flavored yogurt	American Pâté Baby potatoes with grated lemon zest; Milk
American Pâté Steamed broccoli; Milk	Cheese bits Bagel; Juice	Cider House Fish with vegetable Peanut 'n' Jam Squares; Milk
Tiny sandwiches with tomato and basil The Great White Bean; Juice	Kid Fizz	Milk-Free Salmon and Vegetable Fettuccine Spinach Ribbon Salad; Milk

GARDEN GAZPACHO

Gazpacho is an easy, quick soup rich with vegetables. It needs little or no change in order for the entire family to enjoy eating it together. Serve it puréed as a first course or chunky for lunch or supper with bread and cheese.

PREPARATION TIME: 30 minutes
REFRIGERATES: 1 week

2 cloves garlic
1 medium onion, quartered
2 cucumbers, peeled, seeded, and cut into chunks
2 stalks celery, trimmed and cut into 2-inch lengths
3 tomatoes, cored and quartered
1 green bell pepper, cored, seeded, and quartered
1/4 cup fresh lemon juice
Grated zest of lemon
1/4 cup olive oil
1 cup salt-free chicken broth (preferably homemade)

1 quart tomato juice
1 tablespoon chopped fresh dill
10 leaves fresh basil, thinly sliced
1/4 teaspoon ground cumin

1. Place the garlic and onion in a food processor; process until minced. Add the cucumbers and process until smooth. Scrape into a large bowl and set aside.

2. Process the celery, tomatoes, and bell pepper, one at a time, to the consistency you want. Add them to the bowl.

3. Stir in the lemon juice, zest, olive oil, chicken broth, and tomato juice. Season with the dill, basil, and cumin.

4. Cover and refrigerate for at least 3 hours before serving.

MAKES 1½ QUARTS

HEARTY FISH CHOWDER

This hearty and flavorful soup is easy to prepare and a nourishing addition to a young eater's diet.

PREPARATION TIME: 40 minutes
COOKING TIME: 40 minutes
REFRIGERATES: 2 days

3 tablespoons olive oil
2 medium leeks, white part only, rinsed and
   thinly sliced
1 cup salt-free chicken broth (preferably homemade)
3 cups milk
1 smoked ham hock
3 medium potatoes, peeled and cut into 1/4-inch
   dice
1/4 teaspoon dried tarragon
Grated zest of 1 lemon
1 pound fresh or frozen (thawed) fish fillets,
   such as haddock, scrod, or cod

1. Heat the oil in a large saucepan over medium-high heat. Add the leeks and let them cook for 5 minutes. Add the chicken broth, milk, ham hock, potatoes, and tarragon. Simmer uncovered over medium heat for 20 minutes. Add the lemon zest and fish fillets. Simmer until the fish flakes easily and the potatoes are tender, another 15 to 20 minutes. Remove the ham hock and taste for seasoning.

2. To serve to young children, flake the fish checking carefully for bones. Cool slightly.

SERVES 4

ORANGY BAKED CHICKEN

The sweetness of this chicken comes from fresh fruit juice and natural juice concentrate. It keeps the chicken moist during cooking and adds a zesty flavor that children enjoy.

PREPARATION TIME: 20 minutes
COOKING TIME: 45 minutes
REFRIGERATES: 4 days
FREEZES: 1 month

1 medium tomato, cored and coarsely chopped
1 medium onion, thinly sliced
1/2 teaspoon dried thyme
1 chicken (3 1/2 pounds), cut into 8 serving pieces
   and skinned
Juice and grated zest of 1 orange, combined
1/4 cup frozen pineapple juice concentrate,
   thawed

1. Preheat the oven to 350°F.

2. Toss the tomato, onion, and thyme together in a small bowl. Spoon the mixture over the bottom of a shallow casserole just large enough to hold the chicken. Add the chicken pieces, flesh-side up. Pour the orange juice mixture and the pineapple juice concentrate over the chicken.

3. Cover the casserole with aluminum foil and seal tightly. Bake until the chicken is cooked, about 45 minutes. (The breast meat should no longer be translucent.)

4. To serve to young children, remove meat from the bones, and cut into bite-size pieces.

SERVES 4

AMERICAN PATE

Our version of meat loaf gets an extra burst of flavor and nutrition from spinach. For young children, cut the meat loaf into ¼-inch bits. Left over, it is great for lunch.

PREPARATION TIME: 20 minutes
COOKING TIME: 1 hour and 15 minutes
REFRIGERATES: 3 days
FREEZES: 2 months (uncooked)

¾ pound fresh spinach, thoroughly rinsed and
*   stems removed, or 1 package (10 ounces) leaf*
*   spinach, thawed, and squeezed dry*
½ pound ground lean beef
½ pound ground lean veal
½ pound ground lean pork
2 cloves garlic, minced
1 medium onion, diced
¼ cup dry bread crumbs
1 small can (6 ounces) tomato paste
1 large egg

1. Preheat the oven to 350°F.

2. If you are using fresh spinach, rinse the leaves one last time, shake off the excess water, and place them in a heavy medium-size saucepan. Cover and steam over medium-high heat for 4 minutes. Drain, squeezing the leaves as dry as possible.

3. In a large mixing bowl, combine the meats with the garlic, onion, and bread crumbs. Mix thoroughly. Add the tomato paste and egg; mix well. Mix in the spinach.

4. Transfer the mixture to an 8½- × 4½-inch loaf pan. Cover with aluminum foil and seal tightly. Bake for 45 minutes, then remove the foil and bake 30 minutes longer. Let the meat loaf sit for 15 minutes before cutting.

SERVES 4 TO 6

CHEESEY TUNA CASSEROLE

This dish combines the nutrition found in vegetables, protein, and grains. Use small bowties so children from 10 months on can eat them easily with their hands.

   You can prepare this dish ahead and bake just before serving.

PREPARATION TIME: 30 minutes
COOKING TIME: 30 minutes
REFRIGERATES: 5 days
FREEZES: 1 month

2 tablespoons safflower oil or butter
¼ cup all-purpose flour
1 cup milk
1½ cups salt-free chicken broth (preferably
    homemade)
½ pound cheddar cheese, grated
3 cups cooked bowtie noodles
1 large can (12½ ounces) all-white tuna, packed
    in water, drained well
Grated zest of 1 lemon
2 cups lightly cooked broccoli flowerets
1 cup cooked peas (see Note)
1 carrot, peeled and minced or grated
Bread crumbs, for the top
Chopped fresh parsley, for the top

1. Preheat the oven to 325°F.

2. Heat the oil or butter in a medium saucepan.

Add the flour to the pan; stir until well blended. Add the milk and chicken broth, whisking constantly to blend. Continue whisking as the sauce thickens and comes to a boil. When the sauce is quite thick and smooth, remove the pot from the heat. Add the grated cheese, stirring until it has melted.

3. Fold in the noodles, tuna, lemon zest, broccoli, peas, and carrot.

4. Transfer the mixture to a 2½ quart casserole and sprinkle bread crumbs and parsley on top. Bake until the crust turns golden brown, 30 minutes.

SERVES 6

Note: For your toddler's portion, be sure to mash peas.

CIDER HOUSE FISH

This is an easy dish to prepare. For young children, be sure to flake the fish and check carefully for bones.

PREPARATION TIME: 20 minutes
COOKING TIME: 30 minutes
REFRIGERATES: 2 days

1 small yellow onion, cut in half and thinly
    sliced
1 carrot, peeled and grated
1 stalk fennel, rinsed and thinly sliced
2 boneless red snapper fillets (about 1 pound)

1 small apple, peeled, cored, and thinly sliced
1 small pear, peeled, cored, and thinly sliced
Pinch ground cardamom
½ cup apple cider or apple juice

1. Preheat the oven to 325°F.

2. Toss the onion, carrot, and fennel together in a small bowl. Strew a handful on a large sheet of aluminum foil. Place a fish fillet on the onion mixture. Overlap the apple and pear slices alternately across the fish, and sprinkle with the cardamom. Top with the other fillet. Sprinkle the remaining onion mixture over the top fillet. Fold up the sides of the foil and place it on a baking sheet. Pour in the cider or juice, then tightly seal the foil edges to form a packet.

3. Bake the fish for 30 minutes.

4. Remove the baking sheet from the oven, and slit open the foil. (Don't stand directly over the foil; the escaping steam can burn.) Slide the fish onto a serving platter and remove the skin. Pour the juice and vegetables left in the foil over the fish and serve.

SERVES 2

MILK-FREE SALMON AND VEGETABLE FETTUCCINE

B y substituting chicken broth for milk, kids who cannot digest milk can still enjoy a creamy fettuccine dinner.

PREPARATION TIME: 25 minutes
COOKING TIME: 20 minutes

½ pound fettuccine
3 teaspoons olive oil
1 medium carrot, peeled, trimmed, and cut into
   ¼-inch rounds
1 cup broccoli flowerets
¼ pound snow peas, trimmed, stringed, rinsed,
   and cut into ¼-inch-wide strips
1 clove garlic, minced
2 tablespoons all-purpose flour
2½ cups salt-free chicken broth (preferably
   homemade) or bottled clam juice
½ pound cooked fresh salmon, flaked or 1 can
   (16 ounces) salmon, drained and carefully
   picked over
¼ teaspoon dried tarragon

1 tomato, cored and coarsely chopped

1. Bring a large pot of water to a boil. Add the fettuccine and cook until it is tender and not chewy, about 12 to 15 minutes. Drain and rinse under cold running water. Drain again and toss in a bowl with 1 teaspoon of the oil.

2. While the fettuccine cooks, bring another pot of water to a boil and blanch the carrot, broccoli, and snow peas, one at a time, until each is crisp-tender, about 5 to 7 minutes each. When each is cooked, remove with a slotted spoon to a colander, and rinse under cold water. Set aside covered to keep warm.

3. Heat the remaining 2 teaspoons of oil in a large skillet over medium heat. Add the garlic and cook briefly, then stir in the flour whisking constantly until it is well blended. Gradually add the chicken broth. Continue whisking until the broth thickens, about 5 minutes.

4. Add the cooked vegetables, salmon, and tarragon to the sauce.

5. Divide the warm pasta among four plates.

Spoon the sauce over the pasta. Top with the chopped tomato.

SERVES 4

HIGH TIDE SEA SHELLS

S tuffed shells are a great lunch box treat that kids get a kick out of eating. Add leftovers from dinner to the stuffing to get vegetables or protein into the meal.

PREPARATION TIME: 30 minutes
REFRIGERATES: 2 days

1 teaspoon dried tarragon
½ lemon
8 jumbo pasta shells
⅓ cup ricotta cheese
⅓ cup cottage cheese
½ cup grated smoked cheese, such as gouda,
  mozzarella, or mild cheddar
2 small carrots, peeled and grated
1 small cucumber, peeled, seeded, and minced
½ cup cooked peas, mashed
¼ teaspoon dried mint
¼ teaspoon dried basil, or 5 fresh leaves thinly
  sliced

1. Bring a large pot of water with the tarragon added to a boil. Squeeze the lemon half into the pot, then drop it in. Add the shells and boil until they are tender, about 15 minutes. Drain the shells and set aside until cool.

2. Combine the cheeses, carrots, cucumber, and peas. Season with the mint and basil. Spoon the mixture into the shells, then refrigerate until chilled. Wrap each shell individually and send it along as a great play school lunch!

MAKES 8 SHELLS

PITA PIZZA WEDGES

P ita pizzas are quick and easy to make. This is one version. Just about any cooked meats or vegetables will work well.

PREPARATION TIME: 15 minutes
COOKING TIME: 20 minutes
REFRIGERATES: 2 days
FREEZES: 1 month

1 pita bread (5-inches round)
3 ounces smoked turkey, sliced
1 small tomato, cored and thinly sliced
2 fresh basil leaves, cut into thin strips
½ cucumber, peeled, cut in half, seeded, and diced
¼ cup grated mild cheddar cheese

1. Heat the broiler.

2. Place the pita on a baking sheet. Slit it completely around to form 2 circles. Set the top round aside. Place the turkey over the pita bottom, top with the tomato slices, and sprinkle

with the basil. Arrange the diced cucumber over the basil, then the cheese.

3. Broil until the cheese melts, about 7 minutes.

4. Remove from the heat and cover with the pita top. Cut into wedges, and wrap for the lunch box.

MAKES 8 WEDGES

ZUCCHINI PIZZA STRIPS

Z ucchini pizzas cut into finger-size pieces make a great lunch or snack. If you want to get your child to eat more protein, add a little chicken, meat, or tofu under the cheese.

PREPARATION TIME: 15 minutes
COOKING TIME: 25 minutes

1 large zucchini, rinsed and ends trimmed
1 medium tomato, cored and coarsely chopped
1 medium carrot, grated
4 fresh basil leaves, cut into thin strips, or ¼
    teaspoon dried basil
¾ cup grated mozzarella cheese

1. Preheat the oven to 400°F.

2. Cut the zucchini lengthwise into flat strips ¼ inch thick. Bring ½ inch of water to a boil in a skillet. Add the zucchini strips, cover, and cook for 3 minutes. With a slotted spatula, remove the strips to a baking sheet lined with aluminum foil.

3. Sprinkle the zucchini strips with the chopped tomato, grated carrot, and basil. Top each strip with some mozzarella. Bake for 20 minutes, or until the cheese has melted. Let the pizzas cool slightly before serving.

MAKES APPROXIMATELY 5 STRIPS

RED BEAN PIE

Young children do enjoy spicy, flavorful foods like chili. This Mexican-style pie gives you an easy meal with plenty of protein and grains.

PREPARATION TIME: 45 minutes
COOKING TIME: 1 hour
REFRIGERATES: 4 days
FREEZES: 3 months

1 tablespoon safflower oil
2 cloves garlic, minced
1 medium onion, minced
2 ripe tomatoes, cored and coarsely chopped
1 green bell pepper, cored, seeded, and minced
1 pound lean ground beef
1½ tablespoons chili powder
1 tablespoon ground cumin
½ cup tomato purée
1 can (19 ounces) red kidney beans, drained
    and rinsed
1 cup cornmeal
1½ teaspoons baking powder
¾ cup milk
1 large egg
1 cup grated cheddar cheese

1. Heat the oil in a large skillet over medium heat. Add the garlic and onion and cook for 1 minute. Add the tomatoes and pepper; raise the heat to medium-high and simmer for 5 minutes.

2. Add the ground beef, chili powder, and cumin. Stir and cook until the meat has browned, about 10 minutes. (If it renders a lot of fat, drain the meat mixture.) Add the tomato purée and kidney beans, stir to mix. Pour the chili into a 9-inch-deep casserole; set aside while you prepare the cornbread.

3. Preheat the oven to 400°F.

4. Combine the cornmeal and baking powder in a bowl. Stir in the milk and egg, then the cheese. Spread the cornbread mixture over the top of the chili. Bake until the crust turns a nice golden brown, 30 to 40 minutes. Cool slightly before serving to young children.

SERVES 6

THE GREAT WHITE BEAN

Dried beans are a very good source of protein. As a bonus, they absorb the flavors of the broth they cook in, making this a dish both kids and adults will enjoy. The beans get very soft and can be easily mashed for any child over the age of one. This is an excellent side dish with poultry, beef, or sausage.

PREPARATION TIME: 20 minutes
COOKING TIME: 1½ hours
REFRIGERATES: 1 week
FREEZES: 3 months

1 pound dry white navy pea beans
1 quart salt-free beef broth (preferably home-made), or more, if needed
1 quart water
1 ham bone or 2 smoked pork necks or knuckles
¼ teaspoon dried rosemary
2 cloves garlic, minced
1 medium onion, studded with 5 cloves
2 medium carrots, peeled and minced
2 medium tomatoes, cored and roughly chopped

1. Rinse the beans under cold running water, picking through to remove any pebbles.

2. Place the beans in a large pot with the broth and water. Add the remaining ingredients. Bring the liquid to a boil, over medium-high heat. Cover, reduce the heat, and let simmer un-

til the beans are soft enough to mash with a fork, about 1½ hours. Stir occasionally and add more liquid if necessary.

3. Remove the ham bone and discard. Remove the onion; discard the cloves. Slice the onion, return it to the pot, and stir to mix it in. Mash a small portion of the beans for your toddler.

Note: To make bean soup, use 2 to 3 additional cups beef broth and cook until the beans fall apart, another 30 minutes.

SERVES 6

BROWN RICE SALAD

This simple, tasty salad is a deliciously refreshing hot weather dish.

PREPARATION TIME: 15 minutes
REFRIGERATION TIME: 30 minutes
REFRIGERATES: 4 days

2½ cups cooked brown rice (about 1 cup, raw)
1 medium tomato, cored and coarsely chopped
1 cucumber, peeled, seeded, and finely chopped
¼ cup chopped parsley
⅓ cup ground walnuts
⅓ cup fresh lemon juice
2 tablespoons safflower oil
2 tablespoons olive oil

In a mixing bowl, toss the rice with the vegetables, parsley and nuts. Add the lemon juice and oils; toss again. Cover and chill for 30 minutes before serving.

SERVES 6

NUTTED RICE PILAF

Brown rice has more fiber and flavor than white. Since it gets very soft, young children can digest it easily.

PREPARATION TIME: 15 minutes
COOKING TIME: 45 minutes
REFRIGERATES: 3 days

1 cup brown rice
3 cups salt-free chicken broth (preferably home-made)
1 cup water
1 cup ground almonds or pecans
¼ teaspoon ground cloves
Grated zest of 1 orange

1. Preheat the oven to 400°F.

2. Place the rice, chicken broth, and water in a 2-quart ovenproof casserole. Bring the liquid to a boil. Stir in the nuts, cloves, and orange zest.

3. Cover tightly with the lid or aluminum foil and bake in the oven until the rice has absorbed all the liquid and is tender, about 45 minutes.

SERVES 4

EGGPLANT AND CHEESE STACKS

By grilling or broiling the eggplant slices instead of frying them, you don't need to use any oil. Grilling or broiling also give the eggplant a nutty taste. You can serve this to kids under one if you cut it into ¼-inch bits. It reheats well but many like the leftovers served cold.

PREPARATION TIME: 40 minutes
COOKING TIME: 20 minutes
REFRIGERATES: 4 days

1 medium eggplant (about 1 pound), rinsed, trimmed, and cut lengthwise into ¼-inch slices
½ cup cottage cheese
1 cup ricotta cheese
2 large eggs, slightly beaten
½ teaspoon dried oregano
½ teaspoon dried mint leaves
½ dried fennel seeds
2 medium carrots, trimmed, peeled, and grated
½ pound mozzarella cheese, grated
2 medium tomatoes, cored, squeezed of juice, and coarsely chopped

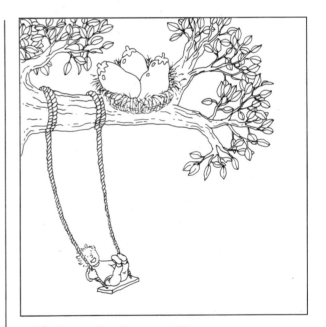

1. Preheat a broiler or grill.

2. Cook the eggplant slices under the broiler or on the grill for 4 minutes. Turn and cook for another 5 minutes.

3. Preheat the oven to 375°F.

4. Drain the cottage cheese to remove excess liquid, about 10 minutes. Place it in a mixing bowl with the ricotta cheese, eggs, herbs, carrots, and 1 cup of the grated mozzarella cheese.

5. Place the eggplant slices in a 9- × 11-inch baking dish or on a baking sheet. Cover each slice with about 2½ tablespoons of the ricotta mixture. Sprinkle the chopped tomatoes on top and then the rest of the grated mozzarella.

6. Bake the eggplant for 20 to 25 minutes. Let it cool before giving it to young children.

SERVES 4

MILK-FREE EGGPLANT CASSEROLE

Don't skip this recipe if your child isn't milk sensitive. It's a very tasty side dish with roasted chicken or steamed fish. If milk products aren't a problem, any bread will do.

PREPARATION TIME: 45 minutes
COOKING TIME: 25 minutes

2½ cups salt-free chicken broth (preferably homemade)
1 large eggplant (about 1½ pounds), peeled and cut into ½-inch cubes
1 tablespoon olive oil
1 small onion, minced
3 slices milk-free bread
2 large eggs

1. Preheat the oven to 350°F.

2. Bring the chicken broth to a boil in a large saucepan. Add the cubed eggplant. If needed, add 1 cup water to cover the eggplant. Return the liquid to a boil. Immediately reduce the heat and simmer uncovered until the eggplant is soft enough to mash, about 25 minutes. With a slotted spoon, remove the eggplant to a bowl. Reserve the liquid.

3. Heat the olive oil in a skillet over medium-high heat. Add the onion and cook until soft, 4 to 5 minutes. Add to the eggplant.

4. Soak the bread slices in about ½ cup of the reserved broth. Let them get good and soggy, then add them to the bowl with the eggplant. Add the eggs and mix thoroughly, mashing and blending the eggplant mixture. Transfer the mixture into a 1-quart casserole.

5. Bake until the center of the casserole is firm and a knife, when inserted, comes out clean, 25 minutes.

SERVES 6

GREEN BEAN PROVENCALE

Green beans make great finger snacks. Cook plenty to have extras in the refrigerator for your hungry child.

PREPARATION TIME: 15 minutes
COOKING TIME: 15 minutes
REFRIGERATES: 3 days

½ pound green beans, trimmed
1½ teaspoons olive oil
1 clove garlic, minced
1 medium tomato, cored and coarsely chopped
¼ teaspoon dried basil
2 teaspoons grated parmesan cheese

1. Bring a pot of water to a boil. Add the green beans and cook until tender, about 7 to 8 minutes. Drain the beans and rinse under cold running water; drain again.

2. Heat the olive oil in a skillet over medium-high heat. Add the garlic and cook for 2 minutes. Add the tomatoes; sprinkle the basil and cheese on top. Toss in the beans and cook just to heat.

3. For children under two, cut the beans into ⅛-inch bits.

SERVES 4

RATATOUILLE

For babies, purée this fine and serve as is, or inside the Snazzy Frittatas (see Index).

PREPARATION TIME: 45 minutes
COOKING TIME: 30 minutes
REFRIGERATES: 1 week

5 tablespoons olive oil
1 medium onion, cut into ¼-inch dice
3 cloves garlic, minced
2 medium zucchini, rinsed, trimmed, and cut into ¼-inch dice

3 tomatoes, cored and coarsely chopped
1 red bell pepper, cored, deveined, seeded, and cut into ¼-inch dice
1 green bell pepper, cored, deveined, seeded, and cut into ¼-inch dice
1 small eggplant (about ¾ pound), peeled, and cut into ¼-inch dice
1 bay leaf
½ teaspoon dried oregano
1 teaspoon chopped fresh dill

1. Place 1 tablespoon of the oil in a large skillet over medium heat. Add the onion and garlic; cook until the onion softens and turns golden brown. With a slotted spoon, remove the onion and garlic to a large bowl.

2. Add 1 tablespoon oil to the skillet. Heat and add the zucchini and toss until it becomes transparent. Transfer the zucchini to the onion mixture.

3. Add 1 tablespoon oil to the skillet. Heat and add the tomatoes. Cook until they take on an orange-yellow color, about 4 to 5 minutes. Transfer the tomatoes to the vegetable mixture.

4. Add 1 tablespoon oil to the skillet. Heat and add the peppers. Cook until they soften, about 4 to 5 minutes. Transfer the peppers to the vegetable mixture.

5. Add the remaining 1 tablespoon oil to the skillet. Heat and add the eggplant. Cook until it is soft, about 10 minutes. If the pan becomes too dry, add 1 to 2 tablespoons water. Test for doneness by tasting a piece. It should not taste bitter. Transfer the eggplant to the vegetable mixture. Add the bay leaf, oregano, and dill. Toss the vegetables. Cover and let sit at room temperature until ready to serve. Remove the bay leaf before serving.

SERVES 6

SQUASHED SQUASH

When yellow squash is steamed, a natural butter flavor comes out that is not found in jarred or dried baby foods. The squash becomes very soft, so you can mash it with a fork for younger children or purée it for infants.

PREPARATION TIME: 10 minutes
COOKING TIME: 12 minutes
REFRIGERATES: 3 days
FREEZES: 2 months

4 medium yellow squash, rinsed and trimmed
1 small onion, cut in half and thinly sliced
½ cup salt-free chicken broth (preferably home-made)

Grated zest of 1 lemon
⅛ teaspoon grated nutmeg

1. Quarter the squash lengthwise and cut each wedge into ¼-inch pieces.

2. Place the onion and the chicken broth in a saucepan; bring to a simmer over medium-high heat. Add the squash, cover, and reduce the heat to medium. Cook until the squash is tender, 10 to 12 minutes.

3. Remove the vegetables to a serving dish and season with the lemon zest and nutmeg.

SERVES 6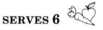

PEAR SALAD WITH YOGURT AND CHEESE

Since ripe pears are soft, they are easy to mash or cut into bite-size pieces for kids of any age. This pear salad makes a good snack.

PREPARATION TIME: 15 minutes

2 ripe pears, peeled, cut in half, and cored
¼ cup grated mild cheddar cheese
2 teaspoons plain yogurt
1 teaspoon mayonnaise

1. Cut the pears into bite-size pieces and divide them between two plates.

2. Sprinkle the cheese over the pears. Mix the yogurt and mayonnaise together; dollop some on each portion.

SERVES 2

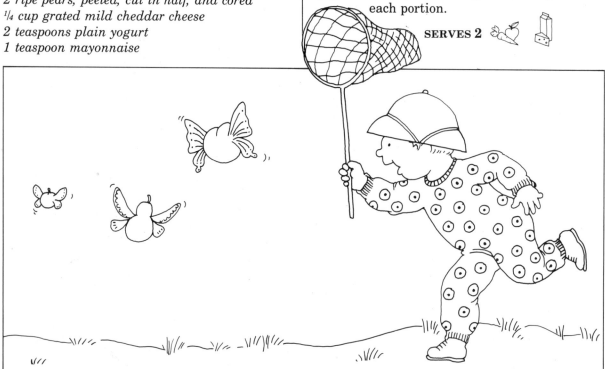

CHAPTER FOUR

Your Child from 18 to 24 Months

B y the time your child reaches 18 months, she has been eating solid foods in some form for almost a year. But now that she has more teeth, she can expand a palate that has been very controlled. Although toddlers are really ready to partake in family meals, they don't necessarily eat them with an adult sense of regularity. Remember that a child will always eat when hungry, so it's better to offer than to force.

Even at 18 months, it is unnecessary to pressure a child into eating a nutritionally balanced meal at every sitting or even within a single day period. It is sufficient if she is satisfied over the course of a week. Pay attention to the foods your child asks for; she may well be satisfying internal body needs, in-stinctively balancing her own diet. By your conscious efforts to offer nutritious foods at both meal and snack times, your child's needs will ultimately be met.

Keep in mind that although your child is eating a more varied selection of foods, her portions should still be a lot smaller than yours. As we've mentioned, a good guideline for approximating a child's serving of meat, fruit, or vegetable is to allow 1 tablespoon for each year of life. Thus, an 18-month-old should get about 1½ tablespoons of apple-sauce or mashed potatoes. Offer this amount and let the child ask for more if she wants it.

Include your child in menu planning and meal preparation. It may help spark an early curiosity in cooking and nutrition. Let her handle food in the kitchen and help choose foods in the supermarket. Plan the family's meals to include liberal amounts of whole-grain or enriched breads and cereals, fresh fruits and vegetables, with moderate amounts of dairy products, lean meat, poultry, fish, and eggs. This will ensure that the whole family is getting appropriate amounts of proteins, carbohydrates, fats, vitamins, minerals, and fiber. Eating this way automatically puts a limit on the amount of fat, sugar, and salt in the diet. Look again to the discussion of the Four Basic Food Groups in Chapters One and Three.

BROWN BAG LUNCHES

At this age, the lunch scene is far from a gourmet dining experience. In order to entice your child to eat, it may require some creativity from the main source—Mom and Dad. You may find that you spend half an hour in the morning assembling what seems a wonderful lunch, only to have a jumbled mess returned to you in the afternoon. Instead, pack small packages of interesting finger foods that your child can pick at, play with, and (with any luck at all) ultimately eat. Try these suggestions:

- Deviled Eggs
  Tuna Sticks (thin finger sandwiches)
  Black olive pieces
  Melon pieces (with or without yogurt)

- Skinned Taters, at room temperature
  Bloomin' Broccoli
  Peanut 'n' Jam Squares.

- Dinner Pickin's (cut-up leftovers like chicken or beef)
  Celery and cucumber spears with Sticky Dip
  The Great Oatmeal Wheel

- High Tide Sea Shells served at room temperature
  Cooked peas
  Steamed Dilled Carrots
  Chunky Pear and Apple Sauce

THE CHUBBY BABY

As we've mentioned before, prevention is the best way to deal with the problem of an overweight child. Be careful that serving portions aren't too large, limit your child's intake of sweets, and encourage active play.

EMERGENCY PACK IDEAS:

Ready-to-drink juice in bottles or boxes
Whole wheat pretzels
Peanut butter/graham cracker sand-
    wiches
Small bags of cereal and chopped raisins
Cubed meats (chicken is a favorite)
Bagels
Cheese sticks
Cut-up fruits (pears, apples, bananas,
    peaches)
Bran Muffins (or other muffin favorites)

Have everything wrapped in child-size
portions. If you are driving, have a box
next to you with all the "goodies" neatly
within reach. You also might have some
"busy-time" activities there as well.

SALTY FACTS

It bears repeating that there is no need to salt
your baby's food. Creative use of herbs, spices,
lemon juice, and other seasonings in these recipes will add to your family's enjoyment of
wholesome foods and limit your need to add salt.

CAUTION FOODS

Although your child can now eat many foods,
the "caution foods"—nuts, olives, popcorn, sunflower seeds, peas, corn kernels, hot dog slices,
chips, pieces of raw carrot or other hard vegetable, grapes, cherries, and raisins—must still
be mashed, chopped, or finely ground.

STROLLING FOODS

You probably question your sanity on the days
you attempt to balance the steering wheel with
one hand and fumble blindly for a toy, a book,
anything to stop the high-pitched wailing of your
pint-size travel companion. Shopping trips in the
stroller are no easier. An "emergency pack" is
a lifesaver we can't praise too highly. Keep one
at hand to get you out of countless frustrating
situations. There will still be some fussing and
restlessness, but you can be fast on the draw
and maintain your fading composure.

Weekly Menu Suggestions: 18 to 24 Months

	Breakfast	Snack
SUNDAY	Poached egg on whole-grain toast; Apple juice	Puréed fruit Plain yogurt with strawberries and bananas
MONDAY	Orange sections Unsweetened cereal with milk	Banana
TUESDAY	Oatmeal Silver Dollars Chunky Pear and Apple Sauce Milk	Vegetables with Sticky Dip Cheese pieces
WEDNESDAY	Open-face toasted cheese Orange juice	Apple Slices
THURSDAY	Fresh fruit salad Yogurt; Orange juice Muffin half	Muffin half Milk
FRIDAY	Peanut butter on whole-grain bread with slices of banana Milk	Strawberries with plain yogurt
SATURDAY	Applesauce Pancakes or French toast Fruit supreme; Milk	Bagel Mashed bananas with plain yogurt

Lunch	Snack	Dinner
Whole wheat bread Peanut butter and fruit- sweetened jam Milk	Orange Muffin Milk	Rosemary Chicken Brown Rice Pilaf Leafy green salad Fruit salad; Milk
Baked Rosemary Chicken bits Steamed Dilled Carrots Bran muffin; Milk	Yogurt with mashed fruit	Sweet Shepherd's Pie Milk

Tuna Surprise on oatmeal or
  whole-grain bread
Apple Slices; Milk
	Cottage cheese with extra
	  chunky Pear and Apple
	  Sauce
		Vegetable Stew
		Whole-grain bread
		Milk

Pastina with Cheese and Vegetables; Milk	Peanut 'n' Jam Square Milk	Brown Rice Paella Leafy green salad; Juice
Welsh Rarebit with Broiled Tomatoes and Broccoli Grape juice	Fresh fruit shake	Steamed Fish Oriental Milk
Surprised-Filled Deviled Eggs Broccoli flowers Juice	Vegetables with Sticky Dip	Milk-free Soufflé with Bloomin' Broccoli Hearty Bread; Milk
Pizza wedges Kid Fizz	The Grand Oatmeal Wheel	Zucchini Lasagna Leafy green salad; Milk

MILK-FREE SOUFFLE

This soufflé is easy to make and very elegant. It makes a nice light dinner.

PREPARATION TIME: 20 minutes
COOKING TIME: 60 minutes

4 tablespoons (½ stick) milk-free margarine or safflower oil
1 medium onion, finely chopped
¼ cup all-purpose flour
1 cup salt-free chicken broth (preferably home-made)
3 large egg yolks
1 teaspoon mustard
1 teaspoon chopped fresh dill
1 medium tomato, cored and coarsely chopped
1 cup grated carrot
½ cup finely chopped smoked ham
5 large egg whites

1. Preheat the oven to 400°F. Coat a 1½-quart casserole evenly and completely with 1 tablespoon of the margarine or oil.

2. Place the remaining margarine or oil in a saucepan over medium-high heat. Add the onion and cook until it is transparent, about 2 minutes. Add the flour and whisk until well blended. Whisk in the broth vigorously until all the flour lumps are gone. Bring the liquid to a boil and let it thicken slightly, about 2 minutes.

3. Scrape this soufflé base into a mixing bowl. Stir in the egg yolks. Add the mustard, dill, to-

mato, carrot, and ham. Mix together well.

4. In a clean bowl, beat the egg whites until they hold a soft peak. Gently fold them into the base just until no white remains. Quickly but gently transfer the mixture to the prepared casserole.

5. Bake in the oven until set, about 50 minutes. Serve immediately.

MAKES ONE 1½-QUART SOUFFLÉ

MILK-FREE CORN CHOWDER

M ost chowders are made with milk or cream, but corn has its own "milk." By steeping the corn in chicken broth, you can produce an incredibly flavorful base. Unlike milky chowders, this one freezes well.

PREPARATION TIME: 20 minutes
COOKING TIME: 50 minutes
REFRIGERATES: 4 to 5 days
FREEZES: 2 months

2 tablespoons safflower oil
1 medium onion, minced
3 tablespoons whole wheat flour
1 quart salt-free chicken broth (preferably homemade)
2 cups corn kernels (scraped from fresh ears when possible), puréed in a blender or food processor
1 cup minced smoked ham
1/8 teaspoon dried tarragon
1/2 teaspoon mustard
1/2 green or red bell pepper, cored, seeded, and finely chopped
Red pepper flakes (for adults)

1. Place the oil in a deep saucepan over medium heat. Add the onion and cook until it is transparent, about 2 minutes. Add the flour and whisk until well blended. Whisk in the chicken broth vigorously until all the lumps of flour are gone. Add the corn, ham, tarragon, and mustard. If you are using fresh corn, add the scraped cobs to the pot. Simmer over medium heat for 45 minutes.

2. Discard the corn cobs. Ladle the chowder into serving bowls and garnish with the peppers. For the adult portions, sprinkle the red pepper flakes over the top.

MAKES 1 QUART

ZUCCHINI LASAGNA

L asagna can be made ahead and frozen, or you may freeze only what is left over. Adding zucchini or any other vegetable, is a good way to sneak an extra vegetable into your child while he eats one of his favorite foods.

PREPARATION TIME: 40 minutes
BAKING TIME: 40 minutes
REFRIGERATES: 3 days
FREEZES: 2 months

4 quarts water
¾ pound lasagna noodles
2 pounds ricotta cheese
2 large eggs
½ teaspoon dried mint
½ teaspoon dried oregano
½ teaspoon dried basil
3 medium (1 pound) zucchini
2 cups homemade tomato sauce, or 1 jar
* (16 ounces) favorite all-natural brand*
12 mushrooms, trimmed and sliced thin
1 pound shredded mozzarella cheese
2 tablespoons grated Parmesan cheese

1. In a large pot, bring the water to a boil; add the noodles. Cook until they are just soft, about 10 minutes.

2. Meanwhile, mix the ricotta cheese with the eggs, mint, oregano, and basil in a large bowl and set aside.

3. Trim the ends off the zucchini and discard. Slice the zucchini, lengthwise, into ¼-inch-thick slices. Set the slices aside.

4. Place the tomato sauce in a medium saucepan and bring it to a simmer over medium heat. Add the mushrooms and continue simmering 5 minutes.

5. Drain the noodles; briefly rinse them under cold water to stop the cooking process; drain again. Lay the noodles flat on a baking sheet.

6. Preheat the oven to 350°F.

7. To assemble the lasagna, ladle ½ cup of the tomato sauce on the bottom of a 9 × 11-inch baking pan. Then alternate layers of noodles, ricotta cheese, tomato sauce, zucchini slices, and mozzarella cheese. Repeat the layers, finishing with the noodles. Top with the remaining sauce and a sprinkle each of mozzarella and Parmesan cheese.

8. Cover with aluminum foil and bake until cooked through and bubbly, 40 minutes. Cool the lasagna before serving it to small children.

SERVES 8

PASTINA WITH CHEESE AND VEGETABLES

This is great for lunch, giving your child foods from all four food groups. To heat leftovers, place the pastina in top of a double boiler over simmering water.

PREPARATION AND COOKING TIME: 25 minutes
REFRIGERATES: 3 days
FREEZES: 1 month

½ cup pastina (small pasta)
1 cup milk
¼ pound muenster cheese, grated or cut into
* small pieces*
2 large eggs
½ cup cooked peas, mashed
½ cup diced cooked carrot
1 medium tomato, cored, and coarsely chopped

1. In a medium pot, bring 2 cups water to a boil; stir in the pastina. Cook until just soft, about 5 minutes. Drain the pastina and set aside.

2. Return the pot to medium-high heat and add the milk. When it begins to simmer, remove the pot from the heat and stir in the cheese, until it melts. Whisk in the eggs. Place the pot over low heat and whisk until the sauce thickens, 5 to 7 minutes.

3. Remove the pot from the heat. Stir in the pastina and cooked vegetables. Cool slightly and serve.

MAKES 4 CUPS

TUNA SURPRISE

This is a quick idea for lunch made with food probably already in your cabinet. Cut the sandwich into tiny pieces so that young children can use their fingers to feed themselves.

PREPARATION TIME: 20 minutes
COOKING TIME: 4 minutes

1 can (6½ ounces) tuna, packed in water,
* drained*
2 tablespoons mayonnaise
2 tablespoons plain yogurt
⅛ teaspoon dried basil
2 slices best-quality whole-grain bread
1 small carrot, peeled, and grated
2 slices (2 ounces) Monterey Jack cheese

1. Preheat the broiler.

2. Mix the tuna fish with the mayonnaise, yogurt, and basil in a small bowl.

3. Divide some of the tuna mixture evenly between the two slices of bread. Sprinkle the carrot shreds over the tuna and cover with a slice of cheese. Place the sandwiches on baking sheets.

4. Broil the sandwiches 2 inches from the heat until the cheese begins to bubble and brown.

5. Allow the sandwiches to cool before cutting into small pieces for children.

MAKES 2 OPEN-FACE SANDWICHES

WELSH RAREBIT WITH BROILED TOMATOES AND BROCCOLI

Although Welsh rarebit is usually served over toast, we've turned it into a more substantial meal by adding broccoli and broiled tomatoes. Try the sauce on pasta, too. Always reheat leftovers in a double boiler.

PREPARATION AND COOKING TIME: 30 minutes
REFRIGERATES: 1 week
FREEZES: 2 months

1 head broccoli, stems trimmed low, and cut into flowerets
½ pound mild cheddar cheese, grated
½ cup salt-free chicken broth (preferably home-made), warmed slightly
¼ teaspoon Dijon-style mustard
1 large egg, slightly beaten
Pinch dried rosemary or basil (optional)
2 ripe tomatoes, cored and cut in half

1. Preheat the broiler.

2. Cook the broccoli in boiling water until tender, about 5 minutes. Drain and set aside.

3. Slowly melt the cheese in the top half of a

double boiler set over simmering water. Gradually mix in the broth. Whisk in the mustard and egg.

4. Sprinkle a little of the rosemary or basil on the cut side of each tomato half. Broil until soft

and beginning to brown, about 5 minutes.

5. Serve the Welsh rarebit over the broccoli and tomatoes.

MAKES 2 CUPS SAUCE

VEGETABLE STEW

S erve this stew as is or use it as a base for cooked chicken or other meat. You might add white navy beans for protein, too. For the toddler in the family, mash the tender vegetables into bite-size pieces.

PREPARATION TIME: 20 minutes
COOKING TIME: 45 minutes
REFRIGERATES: 1 week
FREEZES: 2 months

1 cup dried white navy pea beans (optional)
1 quart salt-free chicken broth (preferably homemade)
2 cups tomato juice
2 medium onions, cut in half and thinly sliced
3 medium potatoes, peeled and cut into ¹/₂-inch dice
4 medium tomatoes, cored and coarsely chopped
4 medium carrots, peeled, trimmed, and cut into ¹/₂-inch slices
1 cup fresh or frozen corn kernels
¹/₄ pound green beans, trimmed and cut into ¹/₂-inch pieces

3 medium zucchini, cut into ¹/₂-inch pieces
1 cup dried small pasta (optional), such as elbow macaroni
¹/₄ cup fresh basil, thinly sliced
1 tablespoon grated Parmesan cheese

1. If you are using the navy beans, bring them to a boil in 4 cups water in a large saucepan. Cover and simmer for 3 minutes. Remove the pan from the heat and allow the beans to sit, covered, for 30 minutes. Drain.

2. Pour the chicken broth and tomato juice into a large soup pot. Add the onions, potatoes, tomatoes, carrots, and navy beans, if using. Bring the liquid to a boil, lower the heat, and simmer, uncovered, until the potatoes are fork-tender, about 25 minutes.

3. Add the corn, green beans, zucchini, and pasta, if using. Season with the basil and Parmesan cheese. Simmer the stew until all the vegetables are tender, about 20 minutes longer. Serve warm with some crusty bread.

SERVES 6

STEAMED FISH ORIENTAL

F ish can be an excellent source of protein, but many children shun it. Try preparing this dish; all the vegetables add interesting flavor to the fish. Leftovers reheat well.

PREPARATION TIME: 25 minutes
COOKING TIME: 20 minutes
REFRIGERATES: 2 days

1 tablespoon safflower or sesame oil
2 teaspoons finely chopped fresh ginger
2 cloves garlic, finely chopped
2 tablespoons rice wine vinegar or apple cider
    vinegar
⅓ cup salt-free vegetable broth (preferably
    homemade) or water
⅙ cup teriyaki sauce mixed with ⅙ cup water
2 tablespoons frozen apple juice concentrate,
    thawed
2 tablespoons tahini (sesame seed paste)
1 tomato, cored and coarsely chopped
1 carrot, peeled and thinly sliced
1 head broccoli, stems trimmed low, and cut
    into flowerets
4 whole scallions, trimmed and sliced length-
    wise
¼ pound snowpea pods, trimmed
1 pound halibut, haddock, or scrod fillets

1. Put the oil in a heavy skillet over medium-high heat. Add the ginger and garlic; stir briefly. Add the vinegar and vegetable broth; stir again. Add the teriyaki sauce; bring the liquid to a boil.

Whisk in the juice concentrate and tahini to make a smooth sauce.

2. Add the prepared vegetables and stir to coat. Cover the skillet and simmer for 7 minutes.

3. Carefully remove the cover. When the steam has cleared, gently place the fish fillets over the vegetables. Replace the cover and cook until the fish and vegetables are done, about 7 minutes.

4. For your child's portion, flake the fish to be sure all the bones have been removed.

SERVES 2 TO 4

BROWN RICE PAELLA

This satisfying one-pot dinner gives you protein, starch, and vegetables along with a little flavor of Spain.

PREPARATION TIME: 20 minutes
COOKING TIME: 1 hour
REFRIGERATES: 3 days
FREEZES: 2 months

2½ cups brown rice
2 tablespoons olive oil
1 chicken (3 pounds), cut into serving pieces, skinned
1 medium onion, chopped
2 cloves garlic, minced
1 can (14 ounces) crushed tomatoes, or 4 medium tomatoes, peeled, cored, and coarsely chopped
1 package (10 ounces) frozen peas, thawed and mashed
5 carrots, peeled and cut into ¼-inch dice
½ pound green beans, rinsed, trimmed, and cut into ½-inch pieces
¼ teaspoon dried rosemary or 3 tablespoons chopped fresh cilantro
5 cups salt-free chicken broth (preferably homemade), slightly warmed
1 pound sole fillets (or any other firm white fish)

1. Preheat the oven to 375°F.

2. Rinse the rice under cold running water, drain, and set aside.

3. Put the oil in a deep, heavy ovenproof skillet over medium-high heat. Add the chicken pieces and cook until browned, about 4 minutes on each side. Remove the chicken to a platter.

4. Add the onion to the skillet and cook until soft, about 2 minutes. Add the garlic; stir and cook 3 minutes longer.

5. Add the rice and stir. Stir in the tomatoes, vegetables, and rosemary. Set the chicken pieces in the rice.

6. Add the chicken broth to the rice mixture. Cover the pan and bake for 50 minutes. Arrange the fish fillets over the rice. Replace the cover, return the skillet to the oven, and bake until the fish is done, about 10 minutes longer.

7. To serve to small children, cut the chicken and vegetables into small pieces. Flake the fish to be sure all the bones have been removed.

SERVES 8

BAKED ROSEMARY CHICKEN WITH TOMATOES

This recipe doubles beautifully. If you do make two chickens, freeze one so you'll be ready for another night. Serve on a bed of brown rice—perfect for absorbing the juices.

PREPARATION TIME: 30 minutes
COOKING TIME: 30 minutes
REFRIGERATES: 3 days
FREEZES: 2 months

1 chicken (3½-pounds), cut into serving pieces
*   and skinned*
¼ cup whole wheat flour
1 tablespoon safflower oil
3 large onions, cut in half and thinly sliced
2 medium garlic cloves, minced
1 teaspoon dried rosemary or 2 teaspoons
*   chopped fresh rosemary*
1 cup salt-free chicken broth (preferably home-
*   made)*
5 large tomatoes, cored and coarsely chopped

1. Preheat the oven to 400°F.

2. Dust the chicken pieces with the flour; set aside.

3. Pour the oil into a large heavy ovenproof skillet over medium heat. Add the onions and cook, stirring occasionally, just until they begin to turn golden, 5 to 6 minutes. Add the garlic and cook for another 2 minutes. Sprinkle in the rosemary.

4. Add the chicken pieces in a single layer and cook until brown, about 4 minutes on each side. Add the chicken broth and tomatoes. Bring the liquid to a boil, cover the skillet, and bake in the oven until the chicken is done, about 30 minutes.

5. To serve to small children, cut the chicken off the bone and into small pieces.

SERVES 3 TO 4

SWEET SHEPHERD'S PIE

If your refrigerator is filled with small amounts of leftover vegetables, this is a delectable way to use them up. The recipe doubles or triples well. Freeze the extras.

PREPARATION TIME: 25 minutes
COOKING TIME: 30 minutes
REFRIGERATES: 4 days
FREEZES: 2 months

3 sweet potatoes, peeled and cubed
1 cup milk
¼ teaspoon ground cinnamon
1 tablespoon safflower oil
3 medium onions, cut in half and thinly sliced
2 cloves garlic, minced
1½ pounds lean ground beef
1 can (16 ounces) crushed tomatoes, or 3 fresh
*   tomatoes, cored and coarsely chopped*
2 cups cooked vegetables such as mashed peas,
*   diced carrots, and diced green beans*
½ cup bread crumbs, or 1 slice of bread, grated
1 package (10 ounces) frozen chopped spinach,
*   thawed*
2 tablespoons apple cider vinegar

1. Preheat the oven to 375°F.

2. Bring a large pot of water to the boil, add the sweet potatoes, and cook until they are fork-tender, about 10 minutes. Drain the potatoes, then mash them with the milk and cinnamon. Set aside.

3. Pour the oil in a heavy skillet over medium-high heat. Add the onions and cook, stirring occasionally, until soft, about 5 minutes. Remove the onion with a slotted spoon to a small bowl, and set aside.

4. Add the garlic to the skillet and cook 2 minutes. Crumble in the ground beef; cook until browned. Drain off the excess fat. Stir in the tomatoes and vegetables, then the bread crumbs.

5. Spoon the meat mixture into a 10-inch round baking pan.

6. Mix the spinach with the apple cider vinegar. Cover the meat with the spinach, and scatter the onions on top. Spread the sweet potatoes evenly over the casserole. Bake until the sweet potatoes begin to brown, 30 minutes.

7. Cool slightly before serving to small children.

**MAKES ONE 10-INCH
ROUND CASSEROLE**

STEAMED DILLED CARROTS

These carrots are great served as a side dish one night and a cold salad the next. You can mix cooked vegetables into many other dishes, such as the Bowtie Pasta Salad (facing page).

PREPARATION TIME: 20 minutes
REFRIGERATES: 1 week

3 medium carrots, peeled and diced
1 tablespoon chopped fresh dill
2 teaspoons apple cider vinegar
1 tablespoon frozen apple juice concentrate,
   thawed

1. Bring 1 inch water in a medium saucepan to a boil. Place the carrots in a steaming basket and set the basket in the pan. Sprinkle the dill over the carrots. Cover and steam until the carrots are tender, about 10 minutes.

2. Place the carrots in a bowl and toss with the vinegar and juice concentrate.

SERVES 3

BLOOMIN' BROCCOLI

Broccoli is a versatile vegetable that can be found fresh all year round. A good source of vitamin C, it can be chopped, puréed, or simply eaten raw.

PREPARATION TIME: 15 minutes
COOKING TIME: 20 minutes
REFRIGERATES: 3 days
FREEZES: 1 month

2 cups salt-free chicken broth (preferably homemade)
2 cloves garlic, minced
1 medium onion, cut in half and thinly sliced
2 tomatoes, cored and coarsely chopped
8 basil leaves, cut into ribbons
1 head broccoli, trimmed and cut into spears
1/4 pound muenster cheese, thinly sliced

1. Preheat the broiler.

2. In a medium-size ovenproof skillet, bring the
chicken broth to a boil. Add the garlic and onion; lower the heat and simmer until they
soften, about 3 minutes. Add the tomatoes and
basil and let simmer for another 5 minutes. Add
the broccoli spears and cover the skillet. Let
cook until the broccoli is tender, 10 minutes.

3. Uncover the skillet and place the cheese slices
over the vegetables. Place the skillet under the
hot broiler until the cheese melts.

4. To serve to a small child, cut the broccoli
spears into bite-size pieces.

SERVES 6

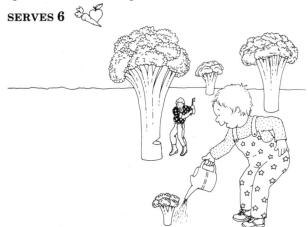

BOWTIE PASTA SALAD

A fanciful salad like this is not only tasty, it
is so colorful that your two-year-old will be
thrilled to find it in his lunch box. This is a good
way to encourage your child to try different
kinds of vegetables.

PREPARATION TIME: 25 minutes
REFRIGERATION TIME: 30 minutes
REFRIGERATES: 5 days

2 cups bowtie pasta
1/2 cup soft-cooked peas, mashed

1 medium carrot, peeled, diced, and cooked
1 cup cooked tiny broccoli flowerets
1 small tomato, cored and coarsely chopped
1/4 cup apple cider vinegar
1 tablespoon frozen apple or orange juice concentrate, thawed
2 tablespoons safflower oil
8 mint leaves, thinly sliced, or 1/2 teaspoon dried
mint
Grated zest of 1/2 orange

1. Bring a large pot of water to a boil. Add the bowtie noodles and cook until just tender, about 10 minutes. Drain; rinse the pasta under cold water; drain again. Put the pasta in a bowl with the vegetables.

2. In a separate bowl, mix together the vinegar, juice concentrate, oil, mint, and orange zest.

3. Toss the vinaigrette with the pasta and vegetables. Refrigerate 30 minutes before serving.

SERVES 4

SKINNED TATERS

T hese little potato skins just might find their way into your hors d'oeuvre selection. Cook them ahead of time, and reheat at a moment's notice, whenever an unexpected guest arrives or your toddler says she's hungry. Pop these in the oven and in a flash all are satisfied!

PREPARATION TIME: 15 minutes
COOKING TIME: 10 to 12 minutes
REFRIGERATES: 3 days
FREEZES: 1 month

2 large potatoes, baked
½ cup plain yogurt
3 medium carrots, grated (about 1 cup)
Pinch curry powder
⅔ cup grated cheddar cheese

1. Preheat the oven to 350°F.

2. Cut the potatoes in half and scoop out the pulp. Reserve it for another meal. Cut each potato skin half into finger-size pieces. Place the skins on a baking sheet and set aside.

3. In a mixing bowl, blend together the yogurt, carrots, and curry powder. Spoon a small portion of this mixture onto each piece of potato skin. Sprinkle some cheese over the filling, place the skins in the oven, and bake until the cheese has melted, 10 to 12 minutes. Let the skins cool slightly before serving them to young children.

MAKES AT LEAST 16 BITE-SIZE TREATS

SURPRISE-FILLED DEVILED EGGS

Deviled eggs are great for the lunch bag or between-meal snacks.

PREPARATION TIME: 20 minutes
REFRIGERATES: 3 days

6 large eggs
2 tablespoons mayonnaise
½ teaspoon mustard
3 tablespoons cottage cheese
½ teaspoon chopped fresh dill
6 black olives, pitted and chopped (about 1 tablespoon)
12 thin slices sweet gherkin pickles

1. Place the eggs in a large pot with cold water to cover. Bring the water to a boil. Boil for 10 minutes, then drain off the hot water. Rinse the eggs under cold running water until they are cool enough to handle. Shell them.

2. Cut the eggs in half lengthwise. Set the whites aside. Place the yolks in a bowl. Add the mayonnaise, mustard, and cottage cheese to the yolks and mash together with a fork until well blended. Add the dill and olives, and mix them into the yolks.

3. Place a sweet gherkin slice in the hole of each white half. Spoon the yolk mixture over the gherkins and serve.

MAKES 12 DEVILED EGGS

STICKY DIP

This is a fabulous dip for steamed vegetables. You might also stuff eggs with Sticky Dip or serve it on wedges of pita. It is truly versatile; everyone in the family will invent his favorite uses.

PREPARATION TIME: 15 minutes
REFRIGERATION TIME: 1 hour
REFRIGERATES: 4 days (Mix thoroughly if the dip has been sitting for any time.)

1 cup cottage cheese
1/2 cup plain yogurt
1/2 cup water-packed tuna (white, preferably solid-packed) drained
1 cup chopped fresh spinach
1 teaspoon chopped fresh dill

1 clove garlic, minced
2 scallions, minced
2 teaspoons frozen apple juice concentrate, thawed
1 teaspoon apple cider vinegar

1. In a mixing bowl, blend together the cottage cheese, yogurt, and tuna, breaking up the chunks of tuna to make a relatively smooth mixture. Add the remaining ingredients and blend thoroughly together.

2. Cover the bowl and refrigerate for 1 hour.

MAKES 2 CUPS

APPLESAUCE PANCAKES

These pancakes have applesauce mixed into the batter, making them sweet and moist.

PREPARATION TIME: 15 minutes
COOKING TIME: 4 to 5 minutes each
FREEZES: 1 month

1/4 cup all-purpose flour
3/4 cup whole wheat flour
2 teaspoons baking powder

1 tablespoon wheat germ
1/2 teaspoon ground cinnamon
1/2 cup frozen apple juice concentrate, thawed
1 cup milk
1 large egg, slightly beaten
1/2 cup steamed Applesauce (see Index) or unsweetened commercial brand

1. In a mixing bowl, blend the flours, baking

powder, wheat germ, and cinnamon together. Stir in the juice concentrate, milk, and egg. Mix thoroughly until blended. Add the applesauce and stir until smooth.

2. Heat a non-stick griddle or pan over medium high heat. For each pancake, ladle ¼ cup batter onto the griddle. When they begin to bubble, after 3 minutes, flip the pancakes over and continue cooking until the undersides are golden brown, about 3 minutes longer.

3. Remove the cooked pancakes to a heatproof plate. Keep them warm in a low oven until you have made all the pancakes.

4. To serve to young children, cut into bite-size pieces.

MAKES TWELVE 3-INCH PANCAKES

MILK-FREE FRENCH TOAST

Using soy or coconut milk makes it easy for the child who can't have cow's milk to enjoy this delicious breakfast treat.

PREPARATION TIME: 7 minutes
COOKING TIME: 5 minutes

1 cup soy or unsweetened coconut milk
2 large eggs
¼ teaspoon vanilla extract
¼ teaspoon ground cinnamon
4 slices milk-free bread

1. In a shallow plate or bowl, whisk together the soy or coconut milk, eggs, vanilla, and cinnamon. Place the bread in the mixture and turn to soften both sides.

2. Place a non-stick pan over medium heat. Add the bread, and cook until brown on both sides, 2 to 4 minutes per side. Serve warm with fresh fruit purée or Applesauce (see Index).

MAKES 4 PIECES FRENCH TOAST

CHUNKY PEAR AND APPLE SAUCE

Fruit sauces are great at breakfast served warm with a little plain yogurt or cereal. This one also tastes great with pancakes and French toast or as a side dish with chicken.

PREPARATION TIME: 20 minutes
COOKING TIME: 15 to 20 minutes
REFRIGERATES: 2 weeks
FREEZES: 2 months

3 McIntosh apples, peeled, cored, and coarsely
    chopped
3 ripe pears, peeled, cored, and quartered
½ cup water
1 tablespoon lemon juice
¼ cup frozen apple juice concentrate, thawed
¼ teaspoon ground cinnamon
⅛ teaspoon ground mace
⅛ teaspoon grated nutmeg

Place all the ingredients in a heavy saucepan.
Bring to a boil over medium heat, then reduce
the heat to a simmer. Cover and cook, stirring
occasionally, until reduced to a chunky sauce,
about 10 minutes. Remove from the heat, cool,
and refrigerate until needed. You can also freeze
in ice cube trays. Keep frozen cubes in a plastic
bag so you can remove one portion at a time.

MAKES 2 CUPS

OATMEAL SILVER DOLLARS

These oatmeal pancakes are a whole-grain treat. If you serve them with fruit sauce instead of syrup, you exchange unnecessary sugar for additional vitamins. Children like silver dollar-size pancakes. They will cook faster, too.

PREPARATION TIME: 2 minutes
COOKING TIME: 15 minutes
REFRIGERATES: 3 days (batter)
FREEZES: 2 weeks (cooked cakes)

1 cup whole wheat flour
1 cup quick-cooking (not instant) oatmeal
2 teaspoons baking powder
¼ cup frozen apple juice concentrate, thawed
2 cups milk
2 large eggs, slightly beaten
Chunky Pear and Apple Sauce (recipe precedes)

1. In a mixing bowl, blend the flour, oatmeal, and baking powder together. Stir in the juice concentrate, milk, and eggs. Mix well.

2. Heat a non-stick or lightly-buttered skillet over medium-high heat. For each pancake spoon ⅛ cup (2 tablespoons) batter onto the skillet. When they begin to bubble, after 2 minutes, flip the pancakes over and continue cooking until

the undersides are golden brown, about 2 minutes.

3. Serve warm with Chunky Pear and Apple Sauce.

MAKES TWENTY 2-INCH PANCAKES

MILK-FREE BANANA PUDDING

Imagine growing up without banana pudding! Here's a recipe for those children sensitive to milk. For variety, add finely chopped walnuts or shredded coconut.

PREPARATION TIME: 30 minutes
REFRIGERATES: 3 days

2 cups unsweetened coconut milk (see Note)
2 tablespoons cornstarch
3 bananas, peeled and roughly puréed
½ cup frozen apple juice concentrate, thawed
3 large eggs, separated

1. Place 1½ cups coconut milk in a saucepan over medium-high heat. Mix the remaining ½ cup coconut milk with the cornstarch; set aside.

2. When the coconut milk is warm, whisk in the banana purée and the juice concentrate. Bring the liquid to a simmer.

3. Whisk the egg yolks with the cornstarch mixture. Vigorously whisk this mixture into the simmering liquid. Continue simmering over medium heat until the pudding thickens. Remove

the pan from the heat.

4. In a clean bowl, beat the egg whites until they hold a soft peak. Fold them into the pudding to lighten it. Pour the pudding into a bowl. Serve immediately or refrigerate.

MAKES 1 QUART

Note: If you use sweetened coconut milk, omit the juice concentrate.

FRUIT SUPREME

This versatile fruit sauce can be served warm over pancakes or French toast.

You might also add ½ cup apple or orange juice concentrate and pour the Fruit Supreme into plastic freezer containers for juice pops. It will take about 45 minutes to freeze. Since there is no sugar in this mixture, they freeze very hard and won't melt too quickly. They make an especially refreshing treat for sore gums awaiting new teeth!

PREPARATION TIME: 10 to 15 minutes
REFRIGERATES: 7 days
FREEZES: 1 month

1 ripe banana, peeled
2 cups strawberries, rinsed and hulled
1 cup fresh (or frozen and thawed) peeled chopped peaches
½ cup steamed Applesauce (see Index) or unsweetened commercial brand
1 tablespoon frozen apple juice concentrate, thawed

Place all the ingredients in a blender or food processor. Process briefly, leaving the fruit roughly chopped. Serve warmed, chilled, or frozen.

MAKES 3 CUPS PURÉE OR
8 TO 10 FROZEN POPS

ORANGE MUFFINS

Keep these small muffins in the freezer so you always have a sweet treat on hand. They thaw out naturally in about 25 minutes. For quicker results, wrap them in foil and place in a preheated 350°F oven for 10 minutes. They are a lifesaving addition to your traveling emergency pack.

PREPARATION TIME: 15 minutes
BAKING TIME: 12 to 15 minutes
FREEZES: 2 months

1 cup whole wheat flour
1 cup all-purpose flour
2 teaspoons baking soda
1¼ teaspoons baking powder
¼ cup powdered milk
¼ cup frozen apple juice concentrate, thawed
¼ cup frozen orange juice concentrate, thawed

Juice of 2 oranges
Grated zest of 1 orange
½ cup water
2 large eggs, slightly beaten

1. Preheat the oven to 350°F. Grease a gem-size muffin tin (1¾ inches wide by ¾ inch deep).

2. In a mixing bowl, blend the flours, baking soda, baking powder, and powdered milk together. Stir in the juice concentrates, orange juice, orange zest, and water. Add the eggs and blend well.

3. Pour the batter into the tins, filling each about ¾ full.

4. Bake until the muffins pull away from the sides of the pan, 12 to 15 minutes.

MAKES 24 SMALL MUFFINS

THE GREAT OATMEAL WHEEL

The tahini in this recipe replaces the traditional butter in batter. These cookies are just one example of the many delicious baked goods that can be made without butter or sugar. If you like your cookies a little sweeter, brush them with the orange glaze. (Because the glaze contains honey, do not serve it to a child under one year old.)

PREPARATION TIME: 20 minutes
BAKING TIME: 17 minutes
FREEZES: 2 months (wrap cookies individually)

½ cup tahini (sesame seed paste)
½ cup frozen apple juice concentrate, thawed
2 large eggs
1 cup quick-cooking (not instant) oatmeal
1 teaspoon baking soda
½ cup whole wheat flour
½ cup all-purpose flour
1 teaspoon ground cinnamon
1 cup finely ground walnuts
½ teaspoon vanilla extract
Orange Glaze (optional; recipe follows)

1. Preheat the oven to 350°F. Lightly butter and flour a baking sheet, or line it with baking parchment.

2. In a mixing bowl, blend the tahini with the juice concentrate. Add the eggs and mix thoroughly. Add the oatmeal and baking soda; mix well. Add the flours and cinnamon; mix again.

Stir in the walnuts and vanilla; incorporate thoroughly.

3. Place generous tablespoons of dough on the baking sheet. Lightly press the dough down with a fork or floured hands. Bake in the oven until golden, 15 to 20 minutes.

4. Remove to a rack. If using the glaze, brush it on the cookies while they are hot.

MAKES 24 COOKIES

ORANGE GLAZE

¼ cup frozen orange juice concentrate, thawed
2 tablespoons honey
2 tablespoons water

In a small bowl, mix all the ingredients together until smooth.

PEANUT 'N' JAM SQUARES

Little gems such as these make a great snack to keep on hand, in an airtight package or in the freezer. Have these healthy treats stashed away, ready for whenever you may need them.

PREPARATION TIME: 20 minutes
BAKING TIME: 35 minutes
FREEZES: 1 month
KEEPS IN AN AIRTIGHT CONTAINER: 1 week

1 cup all-natural chunky peanut butter
¾ cup frozen apple juice concentrate, thawed
2 large eggs
1 cup whole wheat flour
½ cup all-purpose flour
1 teaspoon baking soda
½ teaspoon baking powder
1 cup finely ground unsalted nuts or sesame seeds
½ cup fruit-sweetened jam

1. Preheat the oven to 350°F. Lightly butter and flour an 8-inch square baking pan, using whole wheat flour.

2. In a mixing bowl, blend the peanut butter and juice concentrate together. Add the eggs and blend thoroughly. Add the flours, baking soda, and baking powder to the bowl. Fold in the nuts or sesame seeds.

3. Pat the dough in the prepared pan and spread it evenly. Spread the jam over the dough. Bake until the cake pulls away from the pan, about 35 minutes.

4. When the cake has cooled slightly, remove it from the pan and cut into 1-inch squares. Wrap them in plastic, store in an airtight container, or freeze.

MAKES SIXTY-FOUR 1-INCH SQUARES

CHAPTER FIVE

Your Child from 24 to 36 Months

Turning two opens a brand new door for toddlers. Much to the awe of their parents, children can now express their likes and dislikes far more clearly. It can be tough for parents to deal with this little person's need to demonstrate his independence and individuality. Part of this new found independence may be reflected in a change in eating habits. A child can go through spurts of being *always* hungry, or not the least bit interested in food. Don't insist that your child eat when you want him to. Respect his hunger cycles. If your toddler wants to eat five or six times a day, be flexible and allow it. (Eating several small meals rather than one large one just may help to keep your child lean, too. The body handles calories much better when it gets fewer of them at a time.)

The dinner table often is the scene for many struggles. Your two- to three-year-old will probably be a finicky eater; it is the rare child who goes through toddlerhood without some dietary idiosyncracies. If your child takes to refusing the foods that you offer, all you can do is to keep trying. Don't allow yourself to get caught up in a battle. After an unsuccessful attempt to coax your child to eat breakfast, leave the uneaten portion within reach. He may casually walk over at his convenience and nibble on it. If your child won't touch a vegetable during a meal, make a plate of cut and blanched vegetables (such as carrots, broccoli, and cauliflower) for the afternoon snack. An accompanying small bowl of dip may intrigue him to eat.

If you haven't done so already, let your child help you prepare food. Toddlers are great at pulling the tops off of mushrooms and picking stems off of tomatoes. They can master tearing lettuce in minutes. They love to stir pancake batter. By involving your child, you also are encouraging him to eat. At the dinner table, talk with pride about whatever your child has helped you make. Children will want to taste the food they had a hand in preparing, and your compliments will do wonders for their egos.

As for raising a nutritional saint, forget it! Still, it is your responsibility as a parent somehow to see that your children eat the proper foods so that they will grow and thrive. Look again at our discussion of the Four Basic Food Groups. Remember, too, that dietary quirks aren't the only stumbling blocks on the road to good nutrition. Fighting the television and advertising pressures to indulge in less-than-nutritious foods is a task worthy of Hercules. Despite these influences it *is* possible to get your child to eat well and enjoy it.

WATCH THE PORTIONS

As your child eats more frequently with the rest of the family there may be a tendency to serve her portions that are too large. An average three-year-old needs 1300 to 1500 calories a day, only a few hundred more than a one-year-old needs. Remember that you are feeding a tiny individual who needs lots of nutrients, not many calories. The basic guideline still holds: offer 1 tablespoon of each food served for each year of life. Let your child ask for more if she wants it. Is there such a thing as *too much* of a good food? It *is* possible to over-emphasize milk in a child's diet. Milk is a poor source of iron, so don't allow it to displace iron-rich foods such as lean meats, fish, poultry, eggs, dried peas and beans, and enriched or whole-grain cereals and breads.

ANOTHER WORD ABOUT FATS

After your child turns two, you may want to switch her to low-fat or skim milk. Check with your pediatrician. Don't be zealous in your efforts to control the fat in your child's diet. Young children do need dietary fat to support growth. Even though *you* may be cutting back to minimal amounts of fat in your diet, your child may need more. Again, check with your pediatrician. The American Heart Association recommends that healthy children over age two consume moderate amounts of fat, cholesterol, and salt. You'll find that all our recipes follow these guidelines. We'll show you how minimally sweetened desserts can deliciously replace high-fat, high-sugar candy, cookies, or cake.

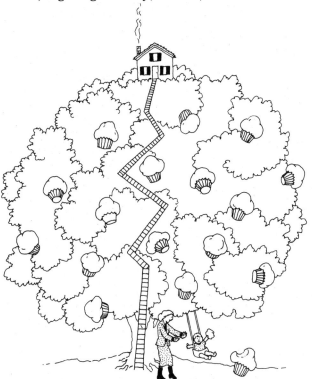

VITAMIN AND MINERAL SUPPLEMENTS

The advice for this age group is the same advice we have been giving throughout the book. If your toddler is healthy and eating a normal diet, there is no need for vitamin and mineral supplements. If you feel your child may not be getting proper nutrition because of erratic eating habits, consult your pediatrician about possible supplements. Do not prescribe them yourself.

SUGAR AND MORE SUGAR

It's almost impossible to avoid sugar because it is added to so many things we eat. Ketchup, mayonnaise, crackers, cereal, peanut butter, and even cough syrup may contain sugar. What's so bad about sugar? Nothing at all, if it's eaten in moderation. The problem is that sugary foods can displace nutritious foods, contribute to overweight, and cause dental cavities. As your child gets older and spends more time away from home, she will be exposed to more influences to eat sugar, whether through television advertising, birthday parties, or well-meaning relatives. And your child will like those sugary foods! What can a nutrition-conscious parent do? Continue to offer homemade baked goods and fresh fruit. If your child requests ice cream or a candy bar, that's okay occasionally but help her understand that other foods are better for us. An occasional foray into the candy bar kingdom is probably a better solution than forbidding a child to have any candy at all. She will get it anyway, so it's best if you are involved.

THE SALTY STORY

As we keep emphasizing, there is no need to salt your child's food. Our recipes are tasty and flavorful, using herbs and spices, lemon juice, sesame seeds, and other seasonings. Once your child acquires a love for salt, it will be a hard habit to break. Prevention is the best approach!

BREAKING THE FAST

An early-in-the-day fueling of our bodies for the day's work or play provides energy and prevents fatigue. Kids are more alert after eating a good breakfast. School may be a few years away, but start encouraging your child now to eat breakfast. Some kids are bored by traditional breakfast fare, so if leftover chicken and rice appeals to your three-year-old at 8 A.M. serve that instead. If that's not your idea of an appropriate breakfast, try not to show your distaste. As long as the food is nourishing and satisfying, it doesn't have to meet any standards of "appropriate breakfast food!" Before giving up on the child who refuses breakfast, try offering a peanut butter sandwich or some leftover macaroni and cheese, tried-and-true solutions. If solid food is the problem, make a shake with milk, fruit, apple juice concentrate, and vanilla extract. That may go down a lot easier! Even the confirmed breakfast-hater will get hungry at some point. Have nutritious food available when your toddler finally shows signs of hunger. If you're going out, take along some cheese and crackers, to satisfy your child's inevitable munchies.

BROWN BAG LUNCHES

Last night's dinner is always the best place to start the search for an easy lunch solution, but other fast or make-ahead ideas include:

- Skinned Taters stuffed with carrots, tomatoes, and smoked ham; bagel pieces, yogurt, and juice
- Cold Chinese Noodles, apple slices, Granola Squares, and milk
- Pita Pizza Wedges, Sweet Banana Dollars, and milk

SHOPPING FOR FOOD

Grocery shopping with your toddler can be an altogether trying experience. The influences of other children and of television will spotlight for your little consumer the endless parade of sugar-filled cereals and snacks on the store shelves. Shopping will become more animated, with pointing fingers and screeches of delight as you pass the boxes your child recognizes. Try to avoid the more dangerous aisles. Reason with your child; the older he gets, the easier this becomes. Before going into the store, tell your child he may pick out one item he wants. Once the selection is made and in hand, you may be able to travel the more questionable aisles with little interruption.

WEEKLY MENU SUGGESTIONS: 24 to 36 MONTHS

	Breakfast	**Snack**
SUNDAY	Great Day Biscuit Scrambled eggs with grated cheese; Milk	Plain yogurt with mashed bananas
MONDAY	Peach and Strawberry Compote with vanilla yogurt Bran muffin; Apple juice	Small cubes mild cheddar cheese Crackers
TUESDAY	Open-faced broiled cheese sandwich; Apple juice	Frozen fruit mousse
WEDNESDAY	Warm oatmeal with Chunky Pear and Apple Sauce Warm milk	Bagel Milk
THURSDAY	Bread pudding with pear purée; Milk	Granola squares Vanilla yogurt with banana
FRIDAY	Poached egg on toast Milk	Cantaloupe pieces
SATURDAY	Stuffed pears with vanilla yogurt; Kid Fizz	Bagel Mashed bananas with plain yogurt

Lunch	Snack	Dinner
Cold Chinese Noodles Apple slices Milk	Bagel Kid Fizz	Chicken Niçoise Summer Zest Potato Salad Spinach Ribbon Salad Fruit Compote; Milk
Creamy Tuna Salad in pita wedges with tomatoes Kid Fizz	Fruit Chewies Milk	Beef and Broccoli Nutted Rice Pilaf; Milk
Beef and Broccoli Boiled potato Milk	Fresh fruit shake Peanut butter on whole-grain bread	Vegetable Fettucine Leafy green salad Apple Snow; Milk
High Tide Sea Shells with tuna flakes Peanut 'n' Jam Squares Orange Juice	Ginger Cookies Milk	Minute Chicken Ratatouille Bread Pudding Milk
Chicken pieces Skinned Taters Milk	Sweet Banana Dollars Kid Fizz	Steamed Cider House Fish Green Bean Provençale Whole-grain bread; Milk

Peanut butter with banana
   purée on toast; Milk
	Small pieces of vegetables with
	   Sticky Dip
		Brown Rice Paella
		Strawberries yogurt; Juice

Brown Rice Paella with
   Caramelized Onions and
   Carrots; Milk
	Frozen Mousse	Beef Stroganoff with noodles
		Wilted spinach; Milk

IMITATING FRIENDS

Around the age of two your child becomes quite the socialite. He will enjoy spending more time with other children, whether in play groups or at their homes. Socialization does have its drawbacks, and imitation is one of them. Your child may see another refuse a food and suddenly decide that he won't like it any more. Feeding can become a game, but staying one step ahead with a solid repertoire of nourishing recipes that blend ingredients and flavors will keep your child's palate from getting bored and often keep him from easily recognizing an ingredient he's decided to dislike.

Another possible drawback to your child's new social standing is that you will have less control over what he is given to eat. If your feel very strongly about what other parents allow their children to eat when your child is visiting, tell them what foods to keep your child away from. Or make up a snack-pack for your child to take with him.

When you take your child to the park or playground, bring snacks and juices with you. That way you won't feel pressured into buying ice cream or soda from a convenient vendor. Your snack-pack can be prepared with homemade sweets so that when your child sees someone else with a cookie, you don't have to say "no," but can offer him a cookie that isn't walloping him with a heavy hit of sugar.

Everything need not be made from scratch. There are good snacks you can buy. Stock snack foods you and your child like to eat, and it will be easier for you to follow through on your good intentions. Some snacks that you can feel good about are:
  Whole wheat pretzels
  Bagels
  Bread sticks
  Low-salt crackers
  Cheerios or other unsugared cereals
  Fruits (bananas can be frozen)
  Plain or homemade fruited yogurt

CAUTION FOODS

Up until the age of three, your child should continue to avoid the same caution foods—nuts, olives, popcorn, sunflower seeds, peas, corn kernels, hot dog slices, chips, pieces of raw or other hard vegetable, grapes, cherries and raisins—unless they are mashed, chopped, or finely ground. Although at this age children may seem able to handle these foods, if they are not chewed properly, they still can become lodged in a young child's throat.

MORE THAN CHUBBY?

If your toddler seems to be getting too chubby, do not put her on a low-calorie diet! As we've said before, look at what "empty-calorie" foods she is eating. Offer lots of fresh fruits and minimally sweetened baked goods to satisfy the sweet tooth. Check serving sizes to make sure they are appropriate, but don't deny your toddler food if she is hungry. Again, we urge you to evaluate your toddler's activity. Is there lots of vigorous play or does your child spend most of the day sitting? If your child is sedentary, encourage more activity.

CHICKEN NICOISE

S ince the chicken in this recipe gets very tender, it is fine to serve to children as young as 12 months if you cut everything into ¼ inch pieces.

PREPARATION TIME: 30 minutes
COOKING TIME: 1 hour

1 chicken (4 pounds), skinned and cut into 8
    serving pieces
¼ cup all-purpose flour
1 tablespoon olive oil
1 medium onion, cut in half and thinly sliced
3 tomatoes, cored and coarsely chopped
2 cloves garlic, minced
½ teaspoon dried oregano
¼ teaspoon dried tarragon
Pinch dried sage
⅔ cup salt-free chicken broth (preferably home-
    made)

16 black olives, pitted and quartered
Nutted Rice Pilaf (see Index)

1. Preheat the oven to 350°F.

2. Coat the chicken pieces lightly with the flour. Heat the olive oil in a large ovenproof skillet over medium-high heat. Add the chicken pieces and cook until brown, about 3 minutes per side. Remove from the skillet and set aside.

3. Add the onion to the skillet. Cook briefly, stirring until the onion begins to brown and soften. Add the tomatoes, garlic, oregano, tarragon, and sage. Add the chicken broth and bring it to a boil. Return the chicken pieces to the skillet along with the olive pieces. Cover and bake for 1 hour.

4. Serve with Nutted Rice Pilaf.

SERVES 4

VEAL STEW

T his is a good dish to make ahead and keep on hand in the freezer. Braising makes the meat so tender, you can easily shred it or cut it into small pieces, and the vegetables in this stew are practically puréed by the time it is ready to be served.

PREPARATION TIME: 25 minutes
COOKING TIME: 45 minutes
REFRIGERATES: 4 days
FREEZES: 2 months

1 tablespoon safflower oil
2 pounds boneless veal, cut into 1-inch cubes
1 tablespoon dried rosemary
6 medium tomatoes cored and coarsely chopped
   or 1 can (28 ounces) tomatoes
2 cloves garlic, minced
1 large onion, cut in half and thinly sliced
2 cups beef broth
1 can (6 ounces) tomato paste
Yogurt Dill Sauce (recipe follows)

1. Preheat the oven to 350°F

2. Heat the oil in a large ovenproof skillet over high heat. Add the veal and cook, stirring occasionally, until browned on all sides. Add the rosemary while the veal cooks. With a slotted spoon, remove the veal and set aside. Add the tomatoes and garlic to the skillet; cook until the tomatoes soften, about 4 minutes. Add the onion, reduce the heat to medium-high, and cook for 8 to 10 minutes. Add the beef broth and tomato paste to the skillet; mix well.

3. Return the meat to the skillet and bring the liquid to a boil. Cover the skillet, transfer it to the oven, and bake until the veal is very tender, about 45 minutes.

4. Serve with Yogurt Dill Sauce

SERVES 6

YOGURT DILL SAUCE

1 cup plain yogurt
3 tablespoon sour cream
¼ cup chopped fresh dill

  Mix all the ingredients together and refrigerate until ready to serve.

MAKES ABOUT 1¼ cups

BEEF STROGANOFF

Serve this stroganoff with Butternut Squash with Grapes. Don't bother puréeing the squash for a two-year-old.

PREPARATION TIME: 30 minutes
COOKING TIME: 30 minutes
REFRIGERATES: 2 days

1 tablespoon plus 1 teaspoon safflower oil
1½ medium onions, thinly sliced

1¼ pounds beef sirloin or rump, cut across the
   grain into ½-inch x ¼-inch strips
2 tablespoons plus 1 teaspoon all-purpose flour
2 cups salt-free beef broth (preferably home-
   made)
¼ cup plain yogurt
3 tablespoons chopped parsley
¾ pound broad egg noodles, freshly cooked
2 teaspoons unsalted butter
¼ teaspoon dried tarragon

1. Heat 1 tablespoon oil in a large skillet over medium heat. Add the onions, lower the heat, and cook slowly until brown, about 15 minutes. Remove the onions from the skillet and set aside.

2. Add the beef to the pan, and stirring continually, quickly sauté until browned all over, about 2 minutes per side. Remove the meat from the skillet and add it to the onions.

3. Add the remaining teaspoon oil to the skillet and heat. Add the flour and whisk to blend. Gradually add the beef broth. Whisk contin-ually until the broth thickens, about 5 minutes.

4. Return the beef and onions to the skillet with the sauce. Cook until heated through. Remove the skillet from the heat, stir in the yogurt, and sprinkle the chopped parsley over the top.

5. Toss the noodles with the butter and tarragon. Arrange them on a platter and spoon the beef over the noodles.

6. To serve to young children, cut the meat and noodles into small pieces.

SERVES 4

BEEF AND BROCCOLI

S erve beef and broccoli with the Nutted Rice Pilaf for a delicious dinner full of protein, iron, and plenty of fiber.

PREPARATION TIME: 45 minutes
COOKING TIME: 20 minutes
REFRIGERATES: 2 days

2 tablespoons plus 2 teaspoons sesame oil
Juice of ½ lemon
1 tablespoon soy sauce mixed with 1 tablespoon water
1 clove garlic, minced
1 tablespoon ginger cut in julienne strips
1¼ pounds beef sirloin or rump, cut across the grain into ¾ inch by ¼-inch strips
1 head broccoli, top cut into small flowerets,
stems peeled and cut into julienne strips
2 teaspoons cornstarch
1½ cups salt-free beef broth (preferably home-made)
1 tablespoon frozen apple juice concentrate, thawed
Nutted Rice Pilaf (see Index)

1. In a bowl, prepare the marinade by whisking together 2 tablespoons oil, the lemon juice, soy sauce, garlic, and ginger. Add the beef and stir to cover with the marinade. Let sit at room temperature for 30 minutes.

2. Bring a pot of water to a boil. Add all the broccoli and cook until tender, about 4 minutes. Drain and rinse under cold running water to stop the cooking process. Drain again and pat dry.

3. In a small bowl, dissolve the cornstarch in a little bit of cold broth. Add the remaining broth and apple juice concentrate and stir to blend.

4. Heat the remaining 2 teaspoons oil in a skillet over high heat. Drain the beef and add it to the hot oil. Stirring continually, quickly sauté the beef until it is browned all over, about 2 minutes per side. Remove the meat from the skillet and set aside. Add the beef broth to the skillet, and let it come to a boil, stirring until it

thickens. Add the beef and the broccoli to the sauce in the skillet, and cook until heated through, 1 to 2 minutes. Serve over Nutted Rice Pilaf. Cut the meat in your child's portion into small pieces.

SERVES 4

MINUTE CHICKEN

A real homemade convenience food—it's very quick and easy.

PREPARATION TIME: 15 minutes
REFRIGERATION (BEFORE COOKING): 2 days
COOKING TIME: 7 minutes

2 boneless, skinless whole chicken breasts, halved
½ teaspoon dried tarragon
Finely grated zest of 1 large lemon
Olive oil, for brushing the grill if used

1. Place each breast half between 2 large sheets of plastic wrap or aluminum foil. Using a meat cleaver or heavy bladed knife, flatten the breasts as thin as you can. The thinner the chicken, the faster it will cook.

2. Sprinkle the tarragon and lemon zest over the chicken pieces. The dish may be prepared ahead to this point. Wrap each chicken piece individually and refrigerate until you are ready to cook.

3. Preheat the broiler or prepare charcoal or wood chips for grilling.

4. When the broiler or grill is hot, lay the breasts on. Cook for 4 minutes, turn and continue cooking for another 3 to 4 minutes. Serve while hot and juicy.

5. To serve to young children, cut the chicken into small pieces or process very briefly in the food processor before serving.

SERVES 4

CHICKEN RAGOUT WITH WHOLE WHEAT BISCUITS

Children enjoy the full-flavored combination of chicken stewed with vegetables. Serve it over a savory-type shortcake.

PREPARATION TIME: 45 minutes (for the ragout)
COOKING TIME: 1 hour
FREEZES: 2½ months
REFRIGERATES: 3 days

1 chicken (4 pounds), skinned, boned, and cut
   into 1½-inch pieces
½ teaspoon dried tarragon
2 tablespoons olive oil
2 tablespoons all-purpose flour
2 cups milk
2 cups salt-free chicken broth (preferably homemade)
2 tablespoon chopped fresh dill
3 carrots, peeled, trimmed, and cut into
   ¼-inch dice
10 cherry tomatoes
1 package (10 ounces) frozen peas, thawed
¼ pound fresh green beans, washed, trimmed,
   and cut into ½-inch pieces
1 package (12 ounces) white mushrooms,
   trimmed
Whole Wheat Biscuits (recipe follows)

1. Sprinkle the chicken with the tarragon.

2. Heat the oil in a large heavy saucepan over medium-high heat. Add the chicken pieces, stirring them around occasionally so that all sides get brown, about 7 minutes. Remove the chicken with a slotted spoon and set aside. Add the flour to the oil in the saucepan and whisk to blend. Whisk in the milk and bring it to a boil. Continue whisking until the milk has thickened. Whisk in the chicken broth and return the mixture to a boil, then add the chopped dill.

3. Return the chicken pieces to the saucepan. Add the carrots, lower the heat, simmer, uncovered, for 25 minutes. Add the tomatoes, peas, green beans, and mushrooms, and continue simmering until all the vegetables are cooked through, 20 minutes more.

4. Serve the stew over freshly baked split biscuits. For very young children, mash or cut up the vegetables as desired.

SERVES 4 TO 5

WHOLE WHEAT BISCUITS

PREPARATION TIME: 20 minutes
COOKING TIME: 25 minutes
FREEZES: 2 months

1½ cups whole wheat flour
⅔ cup all-purpose flour
1 tablespoon baking powder
½ teaspoon caraway seeds
2 tablespoons melted unsalted butter or
  vegetable oil
1 cup milk

1. Preheat the oven to 350°F.

2. Place the flours in a mixing bowl. Add the baking powder and stir to blend. Add the caraway seeds and butter or oil; mix lightly. Add the milk, and mix the dough until well blended.

3. Drop dough by the tablespoon onto an ungreased baking sheet and place in the oven. Bake for 25 minutes. Remove and cool slightly before serving.

MAKES 10 BISCUITS

SUMMER ZEST POTATO SALAD

When golf-ball-size potatoes begin to show up in your grocery, can fresh basil be far behind? Summer is coming, and the fresh seasonal produce blends well in this salad.

PREPARATION TIME: 25 minutes
REFRIGERATION TIME: 30 minutes
REFRIGERATES: 4 days

12 to 16 small new potatoes, scrubbed
2 whole scallions, trimmed and thinly sliced
10 basil leaves, cut into thin strips, or 1 tablespoon dried basil
Grated zest of 1 small lemon
¼ cup plain yogurt
2 tablespoons mayonnaise
¼ cup sesame seeds, toasted

1. Place the potatoes in a pot with water to cover. Bring the water to a boil, and cook until the potatoes are soft, about 15 minutes. Drain the potatoes and run under cold water to stop the cooking process. Drain again and pat dry.

2. Cut the potatoes into ¼-inch chunks and place in a bowl. Add the scallions, basil, and lemon zest. Mix in the yogurt and mayonnaise; sprinkle on the sesame seeds. Mix well. Cover the bowl with plastic wrap and refrigerate for at least 30 minutes before serving.

SERVES 4

COLD CHINESE NOODLES

Chinese restaurants usually welcome children, so most are familiar with oriental flavors like those in this side dish. If your child is under two years old, you may want to use a smaller shape like macaroni so that it will be easy for him to eat with his hands.

PREPARATION TIME: 30 minutes
MARINATING TIME: 1 hour
REFRIGERATES: 3 days

½ pound spaghetti
¼ cup sesame oil
¼ cup tahini (sesame seed paste)
¼ cup all-natural smooth peanut butter
2 tablespoons soy sauce mixed with 2 tablespoons water
2 tablespoons water
1 tablespoon apple cider vinegar or rice wine
⅓ cup salt-free chicken broth (preferably homemade)
2 cloves garlic, minced
1 teaspoon minced fresh ginger
3 whole scallions, trimmed and thinly sliced
2 cups cooked and shredded chicken or beef
1 cup cooked broccoli flowerets
1 tablespoon chopped cilantro (fresh coriander)

1. Bring a large pot of water to a boil. Add the spaghetti and cook until tender, 10 to 15 minutes. Drain the noodles and rinse them under cold running water to stop the cooking process. Drain again and place them in a bowl; toss with 1 tablespoon of the sesame oil.

2. To prepare the dressing, whisk the tahini and peanut butter with the soy sauce mixture and the water in a bowl. Whisk in the remaining 3 tablespoons oil, and the vinegar and broth. Season with the garlic, ginger, and scallions.

3. Toss the noodles with the dressing. Let sit for 1 hour. Just before serving, add the meat, broccoli, and cilantro to the noodles. Toss to combine.

SERVES 6

CREAMY TUNA SALAD

Here's a fast lunch idea that's low in fat and high in protein. Spread this salad on finger-size pita wedges, spoon it over soft-cooked vegetables, use it to stuff pasta shells or hard-cooked egg halves. For a change of pace, use cooked chicken instead of tuna.

PREPARATION TIME: 15 minutes
REFRIGERATES: 4 days (Stir well before serving.)

1 can (7½ ounces) all-white tuna, packed in water, drained well

3 tablespoons plain yogurt
2 tablespoons mayonnaise
10 basil leaves, cut into thin strips
2 tablespoons sesame seeds, toasted

Mix the tuna, yogurt, mayonnaise, basil, and sesame seeds together. Cover with plastic wrap and refrigerate until ready to serve.

SERVES 3

CHICKEN SALAD

Sometimes picky eaters are intrigued by an interesting new food presentation. Try stuffing the chicken salad into pasta shells or cherry tomato halves.

PREPARATION TIME: 15 minutes
REFRIGERATION TIME: 30 minutes
REFRIGERATES: 3 days

2½ cups cooked chicken, cut into ¼-inch cubes
1 cucumber, peeled, seeded, and chopped
¼ cup plain yogurt
2 tablespoons mayonnaise
6 basil leaves, cut into thin strips
1 tablespoon sesame seeds, toasted

1. In a serving bowl, toss the chicken with the cucumber, yogurt, mayonnaise, and basil.

2. Sprinkle the sesame seeds over the salad, cover, and refrigerate for 30 minutes before serving.

SERVES 4 TO 6

SWEET BANANA DOLLARS

Kids have a natural attraction to sweets. Instead of giving them candies with wasted calories, make these banana dollars and keep them in the freezer.

PREPARATION TIME: 20 minutes
FREEZING TIME: 10 minutes
FREEZES: 2 weeks

¼ cup plain yogurt
½ teaspoon almond extract
1 cup ground walnuts, pecans, or almonds
½ pound shredded unsweetened coconut
2 ripe bananas, peeled and cut into rounds,
  ¼-inch thick

1. In a small mixing bowl, blend together the yogurt and almond extract. Set aside.

2. Place the ground nuts and shredded coconut in separate shallow bowls.

3. One at a time dip the banana slices into the yogurt, then roll them in either nuts or coconut. Place them in a pan, cover, and freeze for at least 10 minutes before serving. If not eating immediately, transfer to plastic bags and keep in the freezer.

MAKES 20 DOLLARS

PEACH AND STRAWBERRY COMPOTE

Poaching fruits not only makes them soft enough to mash, they pick up extra flavor from the poaching liquid. Older children might like this compote for breakfast served warm with yogurt. It is also good spooned over Great Day Biscuits.

PREPARATION TIME: 20 minutes
COOKING TIME: 10 minutes
REFRIGERATION TIME: 30 minutes
REFRIGERATES: 1 week

2 cups apple cider or apple juice
1/2 cup frozen apple juice concentrate, thawed
1 cup water
2 cinnamon sticks
6 whole cloves
2 ripe peaches, peeled, cut in half, pitted, and
  sliced
2 pints strawberries, rinsed and hulled

1. In a saucepan over medium-high heat, bring the apple cider, juice concentrate, water, and the spices to a boil.

2. Add the peaches and return the liquid to a boil. Remove from the heat and add the strawberries. Transfer the fruit mixture to a bowl and refrigerate until cool. Serve as is, reheated, or with a dollop of vanilla yogurt.

SERVES 6

FROZEN MOUSSE

If you freeze this mousse in paper cups, it becomes a good snack to take outside. Since the mousse doesn't melt very fast, kids can lick the mousse while pushing it up from the bottom.

PREPARATION TIME: 20 minutes
FREEZING TIME: 1½ hours
FREEZES: 1 week

1/2 cup frozen pineapple juice concentrate,
  thawed
1/2 cup water
2 tablespoons unflavored gelatin
3 cups cubed cantaloupe
3/4 teaspoon almond extract
3/4 cup vanilla yogurt
3 large egg whites

1. To prepare the mousse cups, cut four strips of aluminum foil, each 8 inches long and 2 inches wide. Wrap a strip around the top of each of four 4-ounce paper cups. Secure the foil with tape and set the cups aside.

2. In a heatproof bowl, mix the juice concentrate with the water. Sprinkle the gelatin on the top. Place the bowl in a large saucepan. Add enough water to the saucepan to come halfway up the side of the bowl. Heat over low heat, stirring continually until the gelatin dissolves. Set aside.

3. Chop the cantaloupe cubes coarsely by hand or in a food processor; do not liquefy. Add the almond extract, juice mixture, and vanilla yogurt; stir or process briefly to blend. Set aside in a bowl.

4. Beat the egg whites until stiff but not dry. Gently fold them into the fruit mixture. Divide the mixture among the mousse cups and freeze until firm, at least 1½ hours.

MAKES 4 MOUSSE CUPS

APPLE SNOW

W hen lightly poached, apples make a fresh tasting purée. By using the apples as well as the poaching broth in this recipe, you lose very few nutrients. This light dessert is perfect for any child over one—and adults love it too. Serve it for company with a sauce of puréed fresh or frozen strawberries.

PREPARATION TIME: 40 minutes
FREEZING TIME: 3 hours
REFRIGERATES: 2 days
FREEZES: 2 months

4 McIntosh apples, peeled, cored, and coarsely chopped
1¼ cups water
⅛ teaspoon ground cinnamon
Pinch ground cardamom
⅓ cup frozen apple juice concentrate, thawed
¼ cup frozen pineapple juice concentrate, thawed
1 tablespoon unflavored gelatin
3 egg whites

1. Lightly oil a 1½-quart mold or bowl.

2. Put the apple pieces in a saucepan with 1 cup of the water. Bring the water to a boil, then reduce to a simmer. Add the cinnamon and cardamom and cook, uncovered, over low heat until the apples have turned into sauce, about 25 minutes. Remove from the heat and transfer to a medium-size bowl.

3. Mix the juice concentrates with ¼ cup water in a small heatproof bowl. Sprinkle the gelatin on top. Place the bowl in a large saucepan. Add enough water to the saucepan to come halfway up the side of the bowl. Heat over low heat, stirring continually until the gelatin dissolves.

4. Beat the applesauce with an electric mixer for a few seconds. Then continue to beat while pouring the gelatin mixture into the applesauce in a steady stream.

5. Beat the egg whites in a clean bowl until stiff, but not dry. Fold them into the apple mixture and transfer the mixture into the prepared mold. Freeze for 3 hours.

SERVES 6

STUFFED PEARS

Pears stuffed with grains and fruits and topped with a fruit-sweetened yogurt sauce makes a perfect dessert or snacktime treat. Children also enjoy this dish at breakfast as a welcome change from cereal.

PREPARATION TIME: 20 minutes
COOKING TIME: 40 minutes
REFRIGERATES: Unbaked, 2 days; baked, 4 days

4 ripe pears
¹⁄₃ cup quick-cooking (not instant) oatmeal
¹⁄₄ cup crushed unsweetened pineapple
¹⁄₃ cup chopped walnuts
2 dried figs, minced
¹⁄₄ teaspoon ground cinnamon
¹⁄₄ teaspoon dried mint
¹⁄₄ cup frozen pineapple juice concentrate,
*   thawed*
1 cup apple cider or apple juice
1 cup plain yogurt
¹⁄₄ teaspoon almond extract

1. Preheat the oven to 350°F.

2. Remove the cores from the pears, leaving the bottom ½ inch intact. Set them upright in a baking dish.

3. In a mixing bowl, stir together the oatmeal, pineapple, walnuts, figs, cinnamon, mint, and juice concentrate. Stuff the filling into the cavity of each pear. Pour the apple cider around the

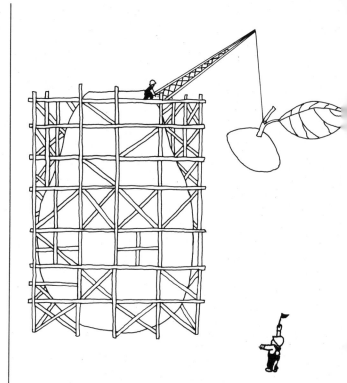

pears, cover with aluminum foil, and bake for 40 minutes.

4. Mix the yogurt, almond extract, and the apple cider that remains in the bottom of the pan together. Spoon over the warm pears.

SERVES 4

BREAD PUDDING

Rich with whole milk and eggs, and spiced with flavor, this smooth custard will be a winner with the entire family. Because it is made with honey, however, don't give this pudding to children under one.

PREPARATION TIME: 35 minutes
BAKING TIME: 1 hour
COOLING TIME: 30 minutes
REFRIGERATES: 2 days

3 teaspoons unsalted butter, room temperature
1 quart milk
3 tablespoons honey
3 large whole eggs
5 large egg yolks
½ teaspoon ground cinnamon
¼ teaspoon ground cloves
Pinched ground nutmeg
1 teaspoon vanilla extract
3 slices whole wheat bread, crusts removed

1. Preheat the oven to 350°F. Butter an oven-proof, 1½-quart casserole, using 1½ teaspoons of the butter.

2. Scald the milk and honey in a large saucepan; remove from the heat and set aside.

3. Place the whole eggs and yolks in a bowl. Add the spices and whisk together. Gradually whisk the egg mixture into the milk. Whisk in the vanilla. Pour into the prepared casserole.

4. Butter the bread using the remaining 1½ teaspoons butter. Float the slices on the custard.

5. Place the casserole into a larger baking pan with high sides. Place the pan on an oven rack and pour enough simmering water into the large pan to reach halfway up the sides of the casserole. Bake until the center of the pudding seems firm when shaken, about 1 hour.

6. Remove the pudding from the water bath and cool to room temperature before serving.

SERVES 6

TAPIOCA SOUFFLE

Most children enjoy a tapioca dessert. Since this recipe is lightened with honey instead of sugar, don't serve it to children under one.

PREPARATION TIME: 40 minutes
COOKING TIME: 30 minutes

¼ cup ground hazelnuts
2 cups milk
⅔ cup quick cooking tapioca
¼ cup honey
1 teaspoon vanilla extract
½ teaspoon ground cinnamon
Grated zest of 1 orange
5 large egg whites
3 large egg yolks

1. Preheat the oven to 400°F. Lightly butter a 1½-quart soufflé mold and dust it with the ground nuts. Set aside.

2. In a saucepan, bring the milk to a boil over medium-high heat. Stir in the tapioca, honey, vanilla, cinnamon, and orange zest; return the milk to a simmer. Cook the tapioca for 3 minutes, stirring constantly. Remove the saucepan from the heat.

3. In a clean bowl, beat the egg whites until stiff but not dry. Beat the yolks into the tapioca mixture, then gently fold in the whites. Transfer the soufflé mixture to the prepared mold and bake until it has puffed and browned, about 30 minutes.

4. Remove the soufflé from the oven and serve immediately, either plain or with a sauce of puréed fruit.

SERVES 6

BROWN RICE PUDDING

Rice pudding is a children's favorite and this version benefits nutritionally from the use of brown rice and a non-sugar sweetener. If you like, add chopped or puréed fruit to the cool pudding.

PREPARATION TIME: 20 minutes
COOKING TIME: 50 minutes
REFRIGERATES: 3 days

3 cups water
¾ cup brown rice
Spiral zest of 1 orange
½ teaspoon ground cinnamon
5 large egg yolks
3 large whole eggs
3 cups milk
½ cup frozen apple juice concentrate, thawed

1. Bring the water to a boil in a saucepan over high heat. Add the rice, orange zest, and cinnamon. Cover the pot and reduce the heat to medium. Cook until the rice is tender, about 45 minutes. Check the water level occasionally to be sure it hasn't boiled dry. Remove the orange zest and discard. Let cook 10 minutes.

2. Whisk the egg yolks and whole eggs together in a mixing bowl. Whisk in ½ cup milk. Stir the remaining milk into the saucepan of rice.

3. Return the saucepan to the heat and bring it to a simmer. Once the milk has begun to simmer, spoon out about ⅓ cup of the hot mixture and whisk it into the eggs to temper them. Pour the egg mixture into the pot with the rice. Whisking constantly, cook the rice mixture until it thickens. Remove the pudding from the heat. Transfer it to a bowl, and chill.

4. When the pudding has cooled, stir in the juice concentrate. (Do not add while the mixture is hot, or the milk will curdle.)

SERVES 4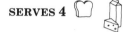

SESAME CRUNCH COOKIES

These cookies will almost always calm a hungry child. Keep them individually wrapped in the freezer or an airtight container. The same mixture will make either cookies or a tart.

PREPARATION TIME: 15 minutes
BAKING TIME: Cookies, 13 to 15 minutes
Tart, 35 minutes
FREEZES: 1 month

½ cup all-natural smooth peanut butter
1 cup frozen apple juice concentrate, thawed
2 large eggs
1⅛ cups quick-cooking (not instant) oatmeal
2 cups sesame seeds
⅔ cup whole wheat flour
1½ teaspoons baking soda
1 teaspoon baking powder
¼ teaspoon grated nutmeg
½ teaspoon ground cinnamon
½ cup chopped dried apples
3 tablespoons apple butter (for the tart)

1. Preheat the oven to 350°F.

2. In a mixing bowl, blend the peanut butter and juice concentrate together. Add the eggs and blend well. Add the oatmeal, 1 cup sesame seeds, the flour, baking soda, baking powder, nutmeg, and cinnamon. Mix thoroughly. Add the apples and mix well.

3. To make the cookies, scoop the dough by generous tablespoons: pat each piece lightly with your hands until it is about ¼-inch thick. Coat each cookie with some of the remaining sesame seeds. Place on a baking sheet, and bake for 13 to 15 minutes. Cool on a rack.

4. To make a tart, lightly butter and flour an 8-inch tart pan. Pat the dough in the pan and spread it evenly. Sprinkle the remaining sesame seeds over the top of the tart. Bake the tart for 35 minutes.

5. Remove the tart from the oven. Spread the apple butter on the top while the tart is still warm. It will melt into an elegant surface.

**MAKES 24 COOKIES
OR ONE 8-INCH TART**

GREAT DAY BISCUITS

PREPARATION TIME: 15 minutes
BAKING TIME: 20 minutes

*1½ cups whole wheat flour
1½ cups all-purpose flour
1 teaspoon baking soda
2 teaspoons baking powder
1 cup milk
¼ cup safflower oil
½ cup frozen apple juice concentrate, thawed
1 cup raspberries or any berry, fresh, or frozen
   and thawed*

1. Preheat the oven to 350°F.

2. In a large mixing bowl, combine the flours with the baking soda and baking powder. Pour in the milk and blend together. Add the oil and juice concentrate. Stir just to mix, then gently fold in the berries.

3. Drop the batter by the tablespoon onto a baking sheet. Bake until golden on top, about 20 minutes.

MAKES 10 BISCUITS

These breakfast biscuits are so good, kids will eat them plain or even stuffed with egg.

APPLESAUCE CAKE

This is a very flavorful and moist cake made without any sugar. Serve it for birthdays or any other special occasions. It will stay moist and fresh for several days.

PREPARATION TIME (INCLUDING ICING): 45 minutes
BAKING TIME: 50 minutes
REFRIGERATES: 3 days

3 large eggs
½ cup vegetable oil
1 cup steamed Applesauce (see Index) or unsweetened commercial brand
1 cup frozen apple juice concentrate, thawed
2¼ cups all-purpose flour
1 tablespoon baking soda
1 teaspoon ground cinnamon
1 teaspoon ground ginger
½ teaspoon ground cloves
1½ cup ground almonds
2 McIntosh apples, peeled, cored, and minced
Apple Butter Icing (recipe follows)

1. Preheat the oven to 350°F. Oil and flour a 9-inch square cake pan. Set aside.

2. Using an electric mixer, beat the eggs until they drop like ribbons from the ends of the blades. Continue beating, adding the oil in a thin stream. Beat in the applesauce and juice concentrate.

3. Beat in the flour gradually until well incorporated. Add the baking soda and spices, then 1 cup of the nuts and the apples.

4. Pour the batter into the prepared pan and bake until the cake sets and pulls away from the sides of the pan, 40 to 50 minutes. Cool on a rack for 15 minutes before unmolding. Let the cake completely cool before icing.

5. Carefully slice the cake in half horizontally. Spread almost half of the icing on the first cake layer, replace the top layer, and cover the top and sides with the remaining icing. Sprinkle the remaining ½ cup ground almonds on top.

MAKES ONE 9-INCH CAKE

APPLE BUTTER ICING

1 package (8 ounces) cream cheese
3 tablespoons fruit sweetened apple butter
2 tablespoons frozen apple juice concentrate, thawed (or to taste)

In a bowl or an electric mixer, beat the cream cheese until soft. Gradually beat in the apple butter and apple juice concentrate. Set aside until ready to ice the cake.

FRUIT CHEWIES

Cookies are always a welcome snack. Baking them without sugar limits empty calories, making the most of what your child eats.

PREPARATION TIME: 30 minutes
BAKING TIME: 30 minutes
HOLDS IN AN AIRTIGHT CONTAINER: 5 days

1 cup all-purpose flour
1¼ cups whole wheat flour
1 teaspoon baking powder
½ teaspoon baking soda
1 teaspoon ground cinnamon
½ teaspoon ground cloves
½ teaspoon ground ginger
¼ cup melted unsalted butter or safflower oil
¾ cup frozen apple juice concentrate, thawed
¾ cup raisins
⅔ cup dried apples
⅓ cup fruit sweetened strawberry preserves

1. Oil and lightly flour an 18-inch long sheet of aluminum foil.

2. In a mixing bowl, combine the flours, baking powder, baking soda, and spices. Stir in the butter or oil and the juice concentrate. Mix thoroughly.

3. Roll the dough out on the prepared foil until about ¼-inch thick. Transfer the foil to a clean baking sheet and refrigerate the dough for 20 minutes.

4. To prepare the filling, chop the raisins in a food processor, until they form a coarse paste. Add the dried apples, and process briefly. Add the preserves, process briefly, and set aside.

5. Preheat the oven to 350°F. Oil and lightly flour a baking sheet. Set aside.

6. Remove the dough from the refrigerator. Cut the dough into three rectangular strips, each about 2 inches wide. Spread some of the filling about 1 inch wide down the center of each strip of dough. With the aid of the foil, close the dough strips over the filling, as you would fold a business letter. Press together slightly to seal. Transfer the rolls to the prepared baking sheet, seam side down.

7. Bake until the crust is golden brown, about 25 minutes. Let the rolls cool for 10 minutes. Using a sharp knife, cut each roll into 1½-inch pieces. Let them cool completely, then store in airtight containers.

MAKES 24 COOKIES

GINGER COOKIES

Kids like to help in the kitchen, especially when the results are as good as these ginger cookies.

PREPARATION TIME: 20 minutes
BAKING TIME: 15 minutes
HOLDS IN AN AIRTIGHT CONTAINER: 4 days

1½ cups all-purpose flour
1½ cups whole wheat flour
1 teaspoon baking soda
1½ teaspoons ground cinnamon
1 tablespoon ground ginger
½ teaspoon ground cloves
1 cup frozen apple juice concentrate, thawed
½ cup unsalted melted butter or safflower oil

¼ cup molasses
1 large egg

1. Preheat the oven to 350°F. Lightly oil two baking sheets. Set aside.

2. In a mixing bowl, combine the flours, baking soda, cinnamon, ginger, and cloves. Stir in the juice concentrate and the butter or oil, then the molasses and egg. Mix well.

3. Drop the dough by the teaspoon on the prepared baking sheets. Bake until the cookies are golden brown, about 15 minutes. Let the cookies cool for 10 minutes before removing them from the baking sheets to a rack.

MAKES 30 COOKIES

INDEX